The National and State Animals of India and their Conservation Status

The National and State Animals of India and their Conservation Status

Professor Madhab Chandra Dash

KALPAZ

First Published, 2018

Published by

Kalpaz Publications
C-30, Satyawati Nagar,
Delhi – 110052
E-mail: kalpaz@hotmail.com
Ph.: 9212142040

Printed at: G. Print Process, Delhi

Cataloging in Publication Data—DK
Courtesy: D.K. Agencies (P) Ltd. <docinfo@dkagencies.com>

Dash, Madhab C., author.
The national and state animals of India and their conservation status / Professor Madhab Chandra Dash.
pages cm
Includes bibliographical references.
ISBN 9789386397416 (HB)

1. Animals—India—States. 2. Wildlife conservation—India. I. Title.

LCC QL84.5.I4D37 2018 | DDC 333.954160954 23

Contents

Preface

India got independence on August 15, 1947 from British Rule and got its constitution on 26 January, 1949 and since then India is a republic. At present India consists of 29 states and 7 union territories. India is an international mega-biodiversity country consisting of about 8 per cent of the total biodiversity of the world, although its land area is about 2.4 per cent of the world's land area. India is rich in biodiversity and has diverse ecosystems and landscapes. These large mammals and some animals are also important for wildlife tourism in India. International tourists visit India to observe wildlife in their natural habitats. The tourism supports the Indian economy.

In recent times, because of enormous population increase, urbanisation, clearance of forest covers for mining, for implementation of developmental projects, and other anthropogenic activities, there is huge loss of biodiversity, especially important wildlife. Many of the wild life are associated with our culture and religion and way of life. Many wild animals are associated with Hindu gods and goddesses. In view of this, wildlife conservation is the call of the day. Indian government has adopted the Bengal Tiger as National Animal and all the states and union territories have also adopted specific animals as their state animal. The important purpose is to sensitize people to conserve these animals so that they will not be extinct in their natural environment like the Indian Cheetah (Acinonyx jubatus).

The purpose of this book is to educate our students, especially school and college students and general public at large to know about National and State animals.

Many books and Wikipedia education services and other documents were consulted to write this book. The photo (most of it taken from wikipedia and other sources) of each animal with a write up on the scientific classification and the conservation status as per IUCN and Wildlife Act of India and their biology and behaviour are described.

I hope this book will serve the purpose for which it is written.

Professor Madhab Chandra Dash

02 October 2017

Chapter - 1

Introduction: The National and State Animals of India

India is a republic and it is made up of 29 states and 7 union territories (Table 1). All Indian states have their own elected government. The Union Territories come under the jurisdiction of the Central Government. Delhi has been allowed statehood with elected assembly but with limited powers. India has a national emblem-The lion capital. Apart from India's national emblem, each of Indian States and Union Territories have their own state seals and symbols which include state animals, birds, trees, flowers etc. To sensitize people about the need of conserving wild life, Government of India is observing wildlife week from October 2, to October 8 every year since 1952. A list of state animals (Table 1) and a write up with photograph of each state animal of India is given in the text of this book.

Table 1. Indian States and Union Territories(?) and Capitals & State Animal

India National Animal 1.Andaman : †	New Delhi Tiger Port Blair State Animal
Andhra Prad	Hyderabad /Amravati (*de facto* from 2017) Blackbuck
Arunachal P	Itanagar Gayal
Assam	Dispur Rhinoceros
Bihar and G	Patna / Panaji OX
Chandigarh †	Chandigarh Indian Grey Mongoose
Chhattisgarh	Naya Raipur -Wild Water Buffalo
Dadra and N †	Silvassa Not named
Daman and I †	Daman Not named
National Ca †	New Delhi Nilgai
Goa	Panaji Gaour
Gujarat	Gandhinagar Lion
Haryana	Chandigarh Blackbuck
Himachal Pr	Dharamshala (W/2nd) Snow leopard
Jammu and I	Srinagar (Summer) Hanglu/Kashmir Stag Jammu (Winter)
Jharkhand	Ranchi Elephant
Karnataka	Bengaluru Elephant
Kerala	Thiruvananthapuram Elephant
Lakshadwee †	Kavaratti Butterfly Fish
Madhya Pra	Bhopal Barasingha
Maharashtra	Mumbai Indian Giant Squirrel Nagpur (W/2nd)
Manipur	Imphal Brow Antlered deer
Meghalaya	Shillong Clouded leopard
Mizoram	Aizawl Himalayan Serow
Nagaland	Kohima Gayal
Odisha	Bhubaneswar Sambar
Puducherry †	Puducherry Indian Palm Squirrel
Punjab	Chandigarh Blackbuck
Rajasthan	Jaipur Chinkara
Sikkim	Gangtok Red Panda
Tamil Nadu	Chennai Nilgiri Tahr
Telengana	Hyderabad Spotted Deer
Tripura	Agartala Phayre's Langur
Uttar Pradesh	Lucknow Barasingha
Uttarakhand	Dehradun Alpine Musk
36.West Bengal	Kolkata Fishing Cat

India is one of the eighteen megadiverse countries of the world; it is home to 7.6 per cent of all mammalian, 12.6 per cent of all avian, 6.2 per cent of all reptilian, 4.4 per cent of all amphibian, 11.7 per cent of all fish, and 6.0 per cent of all flowering plant species. India is home to Asian elephant, Bengal tiger, Asiatic lion, leopard and Indian rhinoceros. These animals are engrained in Indian culture, often being associated with deities. These large mammals are also important for wildlife tourism in India. Many national parks and wildlife sanctuaries also cater to tourism needs.

At present, India's national animal is the beautiful, majestic Bengal Tiger, protected in Sunderban of West Bengal, and many other biosphere and sanctuary. There are several reasons behind it being 'the chosen one' as national animal.The tiger is endangered and needs protection and conservation measures. The tiger has been particularly important, and Project Tiger, started in 1972, was a major effort to conserve the tiger and its habitats. Project Elephant started in 1992 to conserve elephant and for its protection. Most of India's rhinos today survive in the Kaziranga National Park. About 50 per cent of the mammalian species have shrunk in natural distributional range on account of anthropogenic pressures. (ZSI, 2016)

India is home to 428 species of mammals from which 251 species (about 59 per cent) are under the protected/scheduled categories of the Indian Wildlife Protection Act 1972. The 428 species are included in 186 genera, 45 families and 13 orders of mammals, of which nearly 89 species are endangered. Four species namely, cheetah, banteng, Sumatran and Javan rhino are already extinct.

The state animals are those that are native to that region and are mostly endangered/ vulnerable/threatened species. By declaring these animals as the 'State animal', the states ensure that the animals are given special attention for conservation in protected areas as some of them are on the verge of extinction. Indian wildlife Act (1972)- Schedule I animals are endangered animals and other scheduled II, III, IV and V animals are also important for conservation as many of them are vulnerable and adequate data on them are not available. The IUCN categories for conservation purpose are cited below.

IUCN Categories

Ex: Extinct, Threatened: EW (Extinct in the wild), CR (Critically Endangered), EN (Endangered), VU (Vulnerable), NT: Nearly Threatened, LC: Least Concerned.

Indian Wildlife Act, 1972- Schedule I (normally Endangered), Schedule II (May be vulnerable), Schedule III, (in few cases VU, NT), IV, V (Normally not EN,VU, NT).

Ministry of Environment and Forests and Climate Change of Government India and State Government have declared the following National Parks in India.

Table 2: National Parks in India.

Name	*State*	*Established*	*Area (in km²)*	*Schedule Animals*
Anamudi Shola National Park	Kerala	2003	7.50	
Anshi National Park	Karnataka	1987	417.34	The great Indian Hornbill, Tiger, Leopard, Black panther, Bear, Elephant, Deer, etc
Balphakram National Park	Meghalaya	1986	220	Wild water buffalo, Red panda, elephant and eight cat species, including the tiger and marbled cat
Bandhavgarh National Park	Madhya Pradesh	1968	446	1336 species of endemic plants
Bandipur National Park	Karnataka	1974	874.20	Chital, gray langurs, Indian giant squirrel, gaur, leopard, sambar deer, indian elephants, honey buzzard, red-headed vulture
Bannerghatta National Park	Karnataka	1986	104.3	Tiger, sloth bear, peacock, elephant, sambar deer, mouse deer
Betla National Park	Jharkhand	1986	1135	
Bhitarkanika National Park	Odisha	1988	145	Mangroves, saltwater crocodile, white crocodile, Indian python, black ibis, wild pigs, rhesus monkeys, chital
Bison (Rajbari) National Park	Tripura	2007	31.63	
Blackbuck National Park, Velavadar	Gujarat	1976	34.08	Hunting cheetahs, Blackbuck Lodge, the endangered Indian grey wolf, the nocturnal striped hyena, Indian fox, golden jackal, jungle cat and many small mammals like hare, gerbil, field mice, mongoose and hedgehog.

(Contd...)

Buxa Tiger Reserve	West Bengal	1992	760	Tiger
Campbell Bay National Park	Andaman and Nicobar Islands	1992	426.23	
Chandoli National Park	Maharashtra	2004	317.67	
Clouded Leopard National Park	Tripura	2003	5.08	
Dachigam National Park	Jammu and Kashmir	1981	141	Only area where Kashmir stag is found
Desert National Park	Rajasthan	1980	3162	Greatest attraction of the park is a bird called the great Indian bustard, an endangered species found only in India
Dibru-Saikhowa National Park	Assam	1999	340	Known for feral horse
Dudhwa National Park	Uttar Pradesh	1977	490.29	Tiger Panthera tigris, Sambhar Axis axis, Hog Deer Axis porcinus
Eravikulam National Park	Kerala	1978	97	
Galathea National Park	Andaman and Nicobar Islands	1992	110	
Gangotri National Park	Uttarakhand	1989	2390	
Gir Forest National Park	Gujarat	1965	1412	Asiatic lion
Gorumara National Park	West Bengal	1994	79.45	
Govind Pashu Vihar Wildlife Sanctuary	Uttarakhand	1990	472.08	
Great Himalayan National Park	Himachal Pradesh,	1984	754.40	UNESCO World Heritage Site
Gugamal National Park	Maharashtra	1987	361.28	
Guindy National Park	Tamil Nadu	1976	2.82	

(Contd...)

Gulf of Mannar Marine National Park	Tamil Nadu	1980	6.23	
Guru Ghasidas (Sanjay) National Park	Chhattisgarh	1981	1440.71	
Hemis National Park	Jammu and Kashmir	1981	4400	
Inderkilla National Park	Himachal Pradesh	2010	104	
Indra Gandhi Wildlife Sanctuary and National Park	Tamil Nadu	1989	117.10	
Indravati National Park	Chhattisgarh	1981	1258.37	Wild Asian buffalo, tiger reserve, hill mynas
Jaldapara National Park	West Bengal	2012	216	Indian rhinoceros
Jim Corbett National Park	Uttarakhand	1936	1318.5	First national park in India (established in 1936 as Hailey National Park)
Kalesar National Park	Haryana	2003	100.88	
Kanha National Park	Madhya Pradesh	1955	940	
Kanger Ghati National Park	Chhattisgarh	1982	200	
Kasu Brahmananda Reddy National Park	Telengana	1994	1.42	
Kaziranga National Park	Assam	1974	858.98	Highest known tiger density in the World Indian rhinoceros, UNESCO World Heritage Site
Keibul Lamjao National Park	Manipur	1977	40	Only floating park in the world
Keoladeo National Park	Rajasthan	1981	28.73	UNESCO World Heritage Site
Khangchendzonga National Park	Sikkim	1977	1784	UNESCO World Heritage Site
Khirganga National Park	Himachal Pradesh	2010	710	
Kishtwar National Park	Jammu and Kashmir	1981	400	

(Contd...)

Kudremukh National Park	Karnataka	1987	600.32	
Madhav National Park	Madhya Pradesh	1959	375.22	
Mahatma Gandhi Marine National Park	Andaman and Nicobar Islands	1983	281.50	
Mahavir Harina Vanasthali National Park	Telengana	1994	14.59	
Manas National Park	Assam	1990	950	UNESCO World Heritage Site
Mandla Plant Fossils National Park	Madhya Pradesh	1983	0.27	
Marine National Park, Gulf of Kutch	Gujarat	1980	162.89	
Mathikettan Shola National Park	Kerala	2003	12.82	
Middle Button Island National Park	Andaman and Nicobar Islands	1987	44	
Mollem National Park	Goa	1978	107	
Mouling National Park	Arunachal Pradesh	1986	483	
Mount Abu Wildlife Sanctuary	Rajasthan	1960	288.84	
Mount Harriet National Park	Andaman and Nicobar Islands	1987	46.62	Important bird area as attributed by BirdLife International, new species frog named Rana Charles Darwini
Mrugavani National Park	Telengana	1994	3.60	
Mudumalai National Park	Tamil Nadu	1940	321.55	
Mukundra Hills National Park	Rajasthan	2006	200.54	
Mukurthi National Park	Tamil Nadu	2001	78.46	Nilgiri tahr

(Contd...)

Mukundra Hills National Park	Rajasthan	2006	200.54	
Mukurthi National Park	Tamil Nadu	2001	78.46	Nilgiri tahr
Murlen National Park	Mizoram	1991	100	
Nagarhole National Park	Karnataka	1988	643.39	
Namdapha National Park	Arunachal Pradesh	1974	1985.24	
Nameri National Park	Assam	1978	137.07	
Nanda Devi National Park	Uttarakhand	1982	630.33	UNESCO World Heritage Site, UNESCO World Biosphere Reserve
Navegaon National Park	Maharashtra	1975	133.88	
Neora Valley National Park	West Bengal	1986	88	
Nokrek National Park	Meghalaya	1986	47.48	UNESCO World Biosphere Reserve
North Button Island National Park	Andaman and Nicobar Islands	1979	0.44	
Ntangki National Park	Nagaland	1993	202.02	
Orang National Park	Assam	1999	78.81	
Pambadum Shola National Park	Kerala	2003	1.32	
Panna National Park	Madhya Pradesh	1981	542.67	
Papikonda National Park	Andhra Pradesh	2008	1012.85	
Pench National Park[3]	Madhya Pradesh	1977	758	
Periyar National Park	Kerala	1982	305	
Phawngpui Blue Mountain National Park	Mizoram	1992	50	

(Contd)

Pin Valley National Park	Himachal Pradesh	1987	807.36	
Rajaji National Park	Uttarakhand	1983	820	Mainly known for Elephants, Tigers, Leopards and several species of birds, reptiles and Mammals.
Rani Jhansi Marine National Park	Andaman and Nicobar Islands	1996	256.14	
Ranthambhore National Park	Rajasthan	1981	392	
Saddle Peak National Park	Andaman and Nicobar Islands	1979	32.54	
Salim Ali National Park	Jammu and Kashmir	1992	9.07	
Sanjay National Park[4]	Madhya Pradesh	1981	466.7	
Sanjay Gandhi National Park	Maharashtra	1969	104	Bengal Tiger, Asiatic Lion, Indian Leopard, Rhesus Macaque, Bonnet Macaque, Spotted Deer, Hanuman Langur, Indian Flying Fox, Indian Hare, Barking Deer, Porcupine, Palm Civet, Mouse Deer
Sariska Tiger Reserve	Rajasthan	1955	866	
Satpura National Park	Madhya Pradesh	1981	524	
Silent Valley National Park	Kerala	1980	237	Absence of noisy cicadas, hence the name 'Silent Valley'
Simbalbara National Park	Himachal Pradesh	2010	27.88	
Sirohi National Park	Manipur	1982	41.30	
Similipal National Park	Odisha	1980	2750	Tiger, leopard, Asian elephant, sambar, barking deer, gaur, jungle cat, wild boar

(Contd...)

Singalila National Park	West Bengal	1986	78.60	
South Button Island National Park	Andaman and Nicobar Islands	1987	0.03	Dugong, dolphin, water monitor lizard, blue whale
Sri Venkateswara National Park	Andhra Pradesh	1989	353	
Sultanpur National Park	Haryana	1989	1.43	
Sundarbans National Park	West Bengal	1984	1330.12	
UNESCO World Heritage Site				
Tadoba National Park	Maharashtra	1955	625	Tigers
Valley of Flowers National Park	Uttarakhand	1982	87.50	
Valmiki National Park	Bihar	1976	898.45	
Vansda National Park	Gujarat	1979	23.99	
Van Vihar National Park	Madhya Pradesh	1983	4.48	

Chapter - 2

Indian National Animal: Bengal Tiger

(Panthera tigris) IUCN:EN (Endangered), India: Schedue- I, Cites Index I

Indian National Animal: Bengal Tiger (Panthera tigris)
Indian Schedue- I, IUCN:Endangered (EN)

Scientific Classification

Kingdom	:	Animalia
Phylum	:	Chordata
Class	:	Mammalia
Order	:	Carnivora

Family	:	Felidae
Genus	:	*Panthera*
Species	:	*Panthera tigris*

Body Structure

The length of Bengal adult Tiger (=Royal Bengal Tiger- British time) varies fgrom 1.4 to 2.8 meters with a tail measuring about 0.6 to 1.0 meter.The average height at the shoulder of an adult varies between 90 cm to 1 meter and the body weight is about 220 kg.

Ecology

They do not live in group and the social unit is an individual.Their population has shrunk to few thousand only in the wild because of illegal haunting by people. In India they now live in protected areas.Their census is done periodically by counting the pug marks, or by camera or by fitting a radio collar in drugged tigers to determine its home range etc. Bengal tigers are found in India, Bangladesh, Nepal, Bhutan and north-western Myanmar.They are found in tropical deciduous forests and rain forests, mangrove swamps and also in coniferous forests and they love water and can charge into lakes after its prey. They often bathe or cool off in pools and rivers during heat of the day. Adult males usually haunt alone and females haunt alone or with young siblings.

The home range of a mature male tiger may be about 100 sq km in area.The boundary of the home range is usually marked by scent marking. Droppings and scratch marks on trees and boulders.These signals inform other tigers about its sex and size and its territory. It has been accepted that tigers communicate among themselves by roaring and moaning.They protect their territory fiercely against rival males but they may share a part of the territory with females. The white spots behind yhe ears help other tigers in the jungle.

Diet

Their diet is Deer, wild pigs, gaur, buffalo and monkeys.The heavily muscled shoulders, front limbs and strong canine teeth are designed for maximum power to pull down prey. A tiger has excellent eye sight and hearing, which help to track prey usually in the dark.They charge the prey with force and slink on the prey when the distance is within 20 meters. Tigers kill these harbivores by biting the back of the neck or throat of the prey and then drag the prey into thick plant covers to eat. After eating enough, they conceal the carcass of the prey with leaves so that they can return later. An adult tigers feed about 40 kg of meat in one meal and they usually hunt once/twice in a week.

The close relatives of tiger include lion, (Panthera leo persica), Jaguar (Panthera once). Sub-species of Panthera tigris are found in Siberia (Panthera tigris altaica), Sumatra (Panthera tigris sumatrae), Indochina (Panthera tigris corbetti). Caspian region tigers are Panthera tigris virgata.

Reproduction

Males mature in 4-5 years and females in 3-4 years. Their breeding season is from November to April. Male tigers find females by their roar and scent marks and a pair can mate up to 100 times in two days. The gestation period varies from 95 days to 112 days and 2-4 cubs are born in the den of the female. Breeding interval is about two to two and half years. The lifespan is about 26 years in the wild.

The females rear the cubs on her own in the den and the cubs suckle their mother for about six months. However, the cubs start eating meat when they are about eight weeks and they venture outside with their mother. The young ones haunt when they about one year old but stay with their mother until the age of two.

Threats and Conservation

They have been subjected to heavy poaching by human beings. The threat is from human beings for their skin, claws, teeth etc.

The tiger is protected animal in India and the state-wise tiger reserves are listed below. There are 50 tiger reserves in India and these are governed by Project Tiger and administered by the National Tiger Conservation Authority (NTCA). India is home to 70 per cent of tigers in the world. The total number of wild tigers has gone upto 3891 in 2016 according to World Wildlife Fund and Global Tiger Forum. Besides there are many tigers in the Zoos. The tigers are maintained in

53,547.5 km^2 of declared reserves for their scientific, economic, aesthetic, cultural and ecological values and to preserve for all time areas of biological importance as a national heritage for the benefit, education and enjoyment of the people. The National Tiger Conservation Authority of India has a logo, which is reproduced below/

Tiger Reserves of India

Assam

- Kaziranga Tiger Reserve
- Manas Tiger Reserve
- Nameri Tiger Reserve

Arunachal Pradesh

- Namdapha Tiger Reserve
- Pakhui Tiger Reserve

Andhra Pradesh

- Nagarjunsagar-Srisailam Tiger Reserve

Bihar

- Valmiki Tiger Reserve

Chhattisgarh

- Achanakmar Tiger Reserve
- Indravati Tiger Reserves
- Udanti and Sitanadi Tiger Reserve

Jharkhand

- Palamau Tiger Reserve

Karnataka

- Bandipur Tiger Reserve
- Nagarhole (extension) Tiger Reserve
- Bhadra Tiger Reserve
- Anshi Dandeli Tiger Reserve
- Biligiri Rangaswamy Temple Wildlife Sanctuary

Kerala

- Periyar Tiger Reserve
- Parambikulam Tiger Reserve

Madhya Pradesh

- Bandhavgarh Tiger Reserve
- Bori-Satpura Tiger Reserve
- Kanha Tiger Reserve
- Panna Tiger Reserve
- Pench Tiger Reserve
- Sanjay Dubri Tiger Reserve

Maharashtra

- Melghat Tiger Reserve
- Pench Tiger Reserve
- Tadoba Andhari Tiger Project
- Shahayadri Tiger Reserve
- Nagzira-Navegaon Tiger Reserve
- Bor Tiger Reserve

Mizoram

- Dampa Tiger Reserve

Odisha

- Satkosia Tiger Reserve
- Similipal Tiger Reserve

Rajasthan

- Ranthambhore Tiger Reserve
- Sariska Tiger Reserve
- Mukundara Hills Tiger Reserve

Tamil Nadu

- Kalakkad Mundanthurai Tiger Reserve
- Anamalai Tiger Reserve
- Mudumalai Tiger Reserve
- Sathyamangalam Tiger Reserve

Telengana

- Kawal Tiger Reserve
- Nagarjunsagar-Srisailam Tiger Reserve

Uttar Pradesh

- Dudhwa Tiger Reserve
- Pilibhit Tiger Reserve

Uttarakhand

- Corbett Tiger Reserve
- Rajaji Tiger Reserve

West Bengal

- Buxa Tiger Reserve
- Sunderbans Tiger Reserve

In addition to the existing reserves, the National Tiger Conservation Authority has accorded for the creation of four new tiger reserves, and the sites in: Ratapani Tiger Reserve (Madhya Pradesh), Sunabeda Tiger Reserve (Odisha), and Guru Ghasidas Tiger Reserve (Chhattisgarh).

Besides, final approval has been accorded to Kudremukh National Park (Karnataka) for declaring as tiger reserves by States. The State Governments have been advised to send proposals for declaring the following areas as tiger reserves: (i) Suhelwa (Uttar Pradesh), (ii) Mhadei Sanctuary (Goa), (iii) Srivilliputhur Grizzled Squirrel Wildlife Sanctuary/Megamalai Wildlife Sanctuary/Varushanadu Valley (Tamil Nadu), (iv) Dibang Wildlife Sanctuary (Arunachal Pradesh) and (v) Cauvery-MM Hills (Karnataka).

Economic Valuation

An economic valuation of six tiger reserves (Corbett, Kanha, Kaziranga, Periyar, Ranthambhore, and Sundarbans) concluded "that the monetary values of flow benefits emanating from selected tiger reserves range from 8.3 to 17.6 billion annually. In terms of unit area, this translates into 50,000 to 190,000 per hectare per year. In addition, selected tiger reserves protect and conserve stock valued in the range of 22 to 656 billion.

Chapter - 3

The State Animal of Andhra Pradesh, Haryana and Punjab – The Blackbuck

The state Animal of Andhra Pradesh, Haryana and Punjab: Blackbuck (Antelope cervicapra (Linnaeus)) – Indian Schedule I, IUCN category: NT (Nearly Threatened).

A male Blackbuck (Antilope cervicapra)

one male and two females

IUCN	:	LC India Schedule I
Kingdom	:	Animalia
Phylum	:	Chordata
Class	:	Mammalia
Order	:	Artiodactyla
Family	:	Bovidae
Genus	:	*Antilope* Pallas, 1766
Species	:	*Antilope cervicapra*

In India there are only four species of antelopes. They are the (i) Indian Antelope or Blackbuck, (*Antelope cervicapra*), (ii) Chinkara or Indian Gazelle (*Gazella gazelle*), (iii) the four horned Antelope or Chowsingha (*Tetracerus quadricornis*), and (iv) the Nilgai or Blue Bull (*Boselaphus tragocamelus*).

The *blackbuck* belongs to the family Bovidae *and* is known as the Indian antelope, found in India, Pakistan and Nepal. Its generic name originates from the Latin word antalopus ("horned *animal*"). The specific name *cervicapra* is composed of the Latin words cervus ("deer") and capra ("she-goat"). Two subspecies are recognised although they might be independent species: A. c. cervicapra (Linnaeus, 1758) and *A. c. rajputanae* Zukowsky, 1927. The diploid chromosome numbers vary from 30-33.

Body Structure

Blackbuck is a gregarious species, and *lives* in herds of around 5 to 50 individuals, mainly females and young ones, both male and female (fawns). They were once the most abundant hoofed *mammal* on the Indian subcontinent, (Journal of the Bombay Natural *History* Society, 104(2): 178-187). *Blackbuck* is considered to be the fastest *animal* in the world next to Cheetah. The blackbuck can run at as high as 80 kilometers (50 mph) per hour.

The body colour may be black, grayish black and ventral side is white. Albinos are also found occasionally in a herd. There is sexual dimorphism i.e. males are heavy and strong and bear horns. In females, the body colour is often brown and females do not bear horns. Height of males is about 80 cm at the shoulder with a body weight about 40 kg on the average. The average body weight in females is about 27 kg. The horns in males are spiral and measure about 35-75 cm. The white fur on the chin and around the eyes of males is in sharp contrast with the black stripes on the face. The coat of males shows two-tone colouration: (i) while the upper parts and outsides of the legs are dark brown to black, (ii) the underparts and the insides of the legs are all white. On the other hand, females and juveniles are yellowish to tan and the ventral parts are white.

Diet

They graze usually green grass and fruits of *Prosopis juliflora* are often eaten and they eat crops near the human habitation. In summer, food intake is reduced. The blackbuck is a diurnal antelope (active during the day). Blackbuck inhabits grassy plains and slightly forested areas. They need regularly water to drink and therefore they prefer areas where water is available.

Ecology

Three types of typically small groups; (i) the female herds, (ii) territorial males and (iii) bachelor males. Group sizes often fluctuate; depending upon the availability of forage and the nature of the habitat. Herd size reduces in summer due to lack of forage and water.

Reproduction

Males and Females become sexually mature at one-and-a-half years and eight months respectively, but mating does not occur earlier than two years. Adult males may maintain a territory, and mature females are allowed into the territory for grazing. Other males are not allowed into these territories. Territories are marked with scent; using preorbital gland and interdigital gland secretions, faeces and urine .This behaviour is called 'lekking' as a strategy on the part of males to garner females for mating. Territories (1.2 to 12 ha) are established by males on the basis of the locally available of female groups, which in turn is determined by the resource (forage and water) availability. Females often visit these places to forage. The males defend territories from other males, giving out loud grunts and engaging in serious head-to-head fights, pushing each other using horns if necessary. Aggressive display consists of thrusting the neck forward and raising it, folding the ears and raising the tail. The male thus attempts mating with her. Dominant males may try to forcibly copulate with female. The female shows her receptivity by waving her tail and thumping the hindlegs on the ground. This is followed by several mounting attempts by the male, and then copulation occurs. The whole process may last as long as six hours. The female will remain still for some time after copulation, following which she may start grazing. The male may then move on to mate with another female. After mating once, the female can mate again after a month of parturition with the same male or with another male.

Mating can occur throughout the year (more common in February to March and August to October). Gestation period varies from 160 to 180 days; one or two young are born. The average lifespan is about 15 years for males and for females about 18 years in the wild.

Threats and Conservation Efforts

Blackbuck numbers have declined sharply due to excessive poaching, deforestation and habitat degradation. In India, hunting/poaching of blackbuck is prohibited under Schedule I of the Wildlife Protection Act of 1972.

The blackbuck is listed under Appendix III of CITES. In India, hunting of blackbuck is prohibited under Schedule I of the Wildlife Protection Act of 1972. Tigers, wolves, jackles and jungle dogs are the predators. It inhabits several protected areas of India, including the following important areas: Bihar: Kaimur Wildlife Sanctuary Gujarat: Velavadar Wildlife Sanctuary, Gir Forest National Park, Karnataka: Ranibennur Blackbuck Sanctuary; Maharashtra: Great Indian Bustard Sanctuary; Rajasthan: Tal Chhapar Sanctuary, National Chambal

Courtship display in blackbuck

Sanctuary, Park, Tamil Nadu: Point Calimere Wildlife and Bird Sanctuary, Tamil Nadu: Wildlife Sanctuary, Guindy National Park. The blackbuck has been introduced in Texas of United States and in Argentina. The population is USA is about 36,000 and in Argentina is about 9000 (nine thousand). Blackbucks are now extinct in Bangladesh. *Blackbuck* (cervicapra) may be an invasive *animal* in some places such as in Queens land.

Chapter - 4

The State Animal of Arunachal Pradesh and Nagaland: Gayal (*Bos frontalis*)

Gayal (Bos frontalis)

IUCN:

Kingdom	:	Animalia
Phylum	:	Chordata
Class	:	Mammalia
Order	:	Artiodactyla

Family	:	Bovidae
Genus	:	*Bos*
Species	:	*Bos frontalis*

The *Gayal* (Bos frontalis), also known as Mithun, is a large domestic bovine distributed in Northeast India, especially in Arunachal Pradesh and Nagaland, Bangladesh, northern Burma and in Yunnan, China. They are found in Tripura, Mizoram, and Assam. Gayals are mainly found in hill-forests. One hypothesis is that the *Gayal* was domesticated from *wild* gaur (Bos gaurus) in Nagaland; the *animals* are kept semi-*wild*, and live in herds. Another hypothesis is that Gayal is a hybrid descendant (but breeds true) from crossing of wild gaur and domestic cattle, either *Bos indicus* or *Bos taurus*. First description of Gayal was made by Aylmer Bourke Lambert in 1804 and applied binomial nomenclature *Bos frontalis* to a domesticated Gayal probably from Chittagong. In 2003, the International Commission on Zoological Nomenclature retained the same name for the wild species. Most authors have adopted the binomial *Bos frontalis* for the domestic species as valid for wild ones. Phytogenetic by scientists corroborates the taxonomic assessment that the Gayal is an independent *Bos* species originating matrilineally from gaur, zebu and cattle. However, The Gayal differs in several important structural features from the Gaur.

Body Structure

The animal on the average 195 cm tall at the shoulders and weighs about 2,200 pounds (about a ton). The old bulls may be hairless, grayish black, brownish or white and the young one at the time of birth looks light-golden or white in colour. In young *animals* the horns are smooth and polished.

Ecology

They are forest animals and are often seen in wild nearby elephant groups. The wild ones usually feed in the morning and evening and food consists of grasses, bamboo leaves, seedlings, soft parts of bamboo in the growing season. They live in herds of six to 12 animals. Females are usually aggressive when with calves, and there are instances known when people have been severely injured after being gored by one. Male are usually more docile.

Social Importance

The role of the Mithun is associated with livelihood of the people of Nagaland and Mithun management with sago palm harvesting. Some of the domesticated Gayals are white in colour. Gayals play is part of the social life of the people in Arunachal Pradesh. Marriages are fixed after the bridegroom's family donates at least one Gayal to the bride's household. Government of India has established 'The National Research Centre on Gayal-Mithun at Jharnapani, Dimapur, under the Indian Council of Agriculture Research'. At present, the National Research Centre on Gayal-Mithun is functioning for developing the scientific and sustainable rearing system and for catering to the needs of Gayal-Mithun farmers. The mandates are (i) identification, evaluation and characterisation of Mithun germplasm available in India, (ii) conservation and improvement of Mithun for meat and milk. (iii) act as a repository of germplasm and information centre on Gayal-Mithun.

Chapter - 5

The State Animal of Assam: One horned Rhinoceros (Rhinoceros unicornis)

One horned Rhinoceros (Rhinoceros unicornis)- IUCN Category: EN (Endangered), India: Schedule I, Cites: Appendix I.

Earlier it was under Endangered category. India Schedule I, since 1910, Rhino hunting in India became prohibited

Kingdom	:	Animalia
Phylum	:	Chordata
Class	:	Mammalia
Order	:	Perissodactyla
Family	:	Rhinocerotidae

Genus	:	Rhiniceros
Species	:	Rhinoceros unicornis

Indian Rhinoceros unicornis, Kaziranga National Park, Assam, India Species name: *Rhinoceros unicornis*

The Indian Rhinoceros (*Rhinoceros unicornis*) is also called Greater One-horned Rhinoceros and Asian One-horned Rhinoceros and belongs to the family Rhinocerotidae. The word "*rhinoceros*" is of Greek origin; "rhin" meaning "nose", and "ceros" meaning "horn".

The one horned Indian Rhinoceros (Rhinoceros unicornis) is one of the three species of rhinos once found in India. The other two species are now extinct in India and they are the Javan Rhinoceros (*Rhinoceros sondaicus*) and the Asiatic two-horn Sumatran Rhinoceros (Didermocerus *sumatrensis*).

Body Structure

Rhinoceros unicornis has a thick grey-brown skin with pinkish skin folds and the horn is black. Its upper legs and shoulders are covered in wart-like bumps. Wart-like bumps are also found on the hind legs. Indian Rhinoceros has very little body hair, aside from eyelashes, ear fringes and tail brush. Males have huge neck folds. *Rhinoceros unicornis stands over on the average 180 cm in height at the shoulder and the thick skin folded behind the shoulders and front of the thighs. The average length of the adult animal is about 10-12 feet and the body weight is about two tons. Males have larger body size and body weight than females. Both males and females bear horn emerging from the skin near the nose and the horn measures about 25- 40 cm.* The average body weight of male is about 2,200 kg and it is heavier than the female, which has an average body weight of about 1,600 kg. The horn is frequently worn down to a thick knob. The horn is made up of keratin. New born young ones do not bear horns. Rhino's skull is heavy with a basal length above 60 cm and an occipital region is above 19 cm. The body weight of largest-sized Rhinos range up to 4,000 kg.

Ecology

The large mammal is primarily found in Assam and parts of north-eastern India. The populations are confined to the Riverine grasslands in the foothills of the eastern Himalayas. The Indian rhinoceros once were found throughout the entire stretch of the Indo-Gangetic Plain, but reduction of their natural habitat drastically and excessive hunting for their horn, the population has been reduced. *Once the animal was found in Uttar Pradesh, West Bengal, Assam and Nepal. At present the distribution is confined to Brahmaputra River Valley in Assam (Kaziranga Wildlife Sanctuary), and in two reserve forests in West Bengal. The Indian Rhino is larger than the African black Rhinoceros and smaller than the African white Rhinoceros.* Rhinos have excellent senses of hearing and smell, but relatively poor eyesight. They can run at speeds of up to 55 km/h for short period in day time.

Indian rhinos are often friendly and often greet each other by waving or bobbing their heads, nuzzling noses, or licking. Rhinos will playfully period, run around, and play with twigs in their mouths. Adult males are the primary instigators in fights. Indian rhino fights with its incisors, rather than its horns whereas African Rhino use horns during fight.

Individuals congregate at bathing site. They also form short-term groupings, particularly at forest wallows during the monsoon season and in grasslands during March and April. Groups of up to ten rhinos, typically a dominant male with females and calves, but normally no sub-adult males remain in such groups. They bathe regularly. The folds in their skin trap water and hold it even when they come back on land. They are active from dusk to early morning. Rhinos spend the day wallowing in water bodies namely, lakes, rivers, and ponds, to cool down and also graze there on aquatic plants. They are excellent swimmers. Egrets and Mynahs both eat invertebrates from the rhino's skin and around its feet and both are Commensals.

Fossils of *R. unicornis* appear in the Middle Pleistocene. The Indian and Javan rhinoceroses, first appeared in the fossil record in Asia around 1.6 million–3.3 million years ago. They occurred throughout South and Southeast Asia. Fossil specimens have also been located in Sri Lanka. In Holocene, until as recently as 3,200 years ago, some rhinoceros lived in Gujarat and Pakistan.

Diet

Indian rhinoceros are grazers and their diets consist of grasses, leaves, branches of shrubs and trees, fruits, and submerged and floating aquatic plants. They feed in the mornings and evenings. They have prehensile lips and they use it to grasp grass stems, bend the stem down, bite off the top, and then eat the grass. They tackle very tall grasses or saplings by walking over the plant, with legs on both sides use their body weight to push the end of the plant down to the level of the mouth. Mothers use this technique to make food edible for their calves. Rhinos drink for a minute or two at a time.

Reproductive Behaviour

The Indian rhino females remain with calves and the male is mostly solitary with the exception of breeding pairs in the breeding season. Dominant males have home ranges of around 2 to 8 km^2 and may overlap with other males. Dominant males tolerate other males passing through their territories but do not tolerate in mating season, and often fights break out. They are generally solitary, except for mating and fighting. Fights between dominant males are the most common cause of rhino mortality. Males are also very aggressive toward females during courtship. Males will chase females over long distances for mating and even attack them face-to-face. Mothers stay close to their calves for up to four years after their birth, sometimes allowing an older calf to continue to accompany her once a newborn calf arrives. Sub-adult males and females may form consistent groupings. Groups of two or three young males will often form a group on the edge of the home ranges of dominant males, presumably for their protection from the dominant male. Rhino babies on the average weigh about 39 kg.

At least 10 distinct vocalisations have been identified in Indian rhinos: snorting, honking, bleating, roaring, squeak-panting, moo-grunting, shrieking, groaning, rumbling, and humphing. In addition to noises, the rhino uses olfactory communication. The significance of vocalisation to sexual activity is not known. Males have been observed walking with their heads to the ground as if sniffing, presumably following the scent of females. Adult males urinate backwards, as far as 3–4 m behind them, often in response to being disturbed by observers. The Indian rhinoceros often defecates near other large dung piles and have pedal scent glands which are used to mark their presence at dung piles. Captive females breed as young as four years of age, but in the wild, they usually start breeding only when six years old, which likely indicates they need to be large enough to avoid being killed by aggressive males. Their gestation period is around 15.7 months, and birth interval ranges from 34–51 months. Captive males and females breed at five years and six years of age respectively. Wild males attain sexual maturity much later when they are larger. The life span is known to be 40-47 years.

Threats to Rhino Population and Conservation Measures

The natural enemies of rhino-calves are the tigers. Adult rhinos, because of their size are not vulnerable to predators. Female rhinos normally protect the calves. The rhinos are also vulnerable to diseases spread by leeches, ticks, and nematodes parasites. Anthrax and the blood-disease septicemia are known to occur in them. *Tabanus* flies, a type of horse-fly, are known to bite rhinos. Tigers are known to hunt singly and not in groups. But in March 2017, four tigers consisting of an adult male, adult female and two cubs together killed a 20-year old male rhino in the Dudhwa Tiger Reserve (wikipedia). Humans hunt them for the horn, believed to have aphrodisiac property. Invasion of few alien grass species into the grazing site and competition for grazing with domestic cattle are other reasons for decline in population.

It is believed by the people that the horn, blood and urine of the Rhino have aphrodisiac properties and therefore it was poached heavily. It is now a protected animal. About 3,000 rhinos live in the wild at present and 2,000 of which are found in Assam alone. (Source: Wikipedia).The Indian *rhinoceros* (*Rhinoceros unicornis*), is also called the greater one-horned *rhinoceros*. The Indian *rhinoceros* is second in size only to the Asian *elephant.*

In 2006, the total population was estimated to be 2,575 individuals, of which 2,200 lived in Indian protected areas. The present estimate is that about 3000 rhinos are found in India. The protected areas are the following: (i) Kaziranga National Park, (ii) Jaldapara National Park, (iii) Pobitora Wildlife Sanctuary, (iv) Orang National Park, (v) Gorumara, (vi) Dudhwa National Park, (vii) Manas National Park,

(viii) Katarniaghat Wildlife Sanctuary. Sport hunting became common during British period. In the 1800s and 1900s, Indian rhinos were hunted by British officers and Indian kings regularly. Reports from the middle of the nineteenth century claim that some British military officers in Assam individually shot more than 200 rhinos and by 1908, the population in Kaziranga had decreased, to near extinction to around 12 individuals. Even after enactment of Indian Wildlife Act, in 1972, Poaching for rhinoceros horn for traditional Chinese medicine and aphrodisiac use became the single most important reason for the decline of the population. Shooting, Trapping, Electrocution, Spearing, Using noose to strangulate the animal and Poisoning by zinc phosphide; pesticides are the most common method used by rhino horn traders. The population has now built up due to strict conservation measures were put in place from the beginning of the twentieth century.

Chapter - 6

The State Animal of Bihar: OX

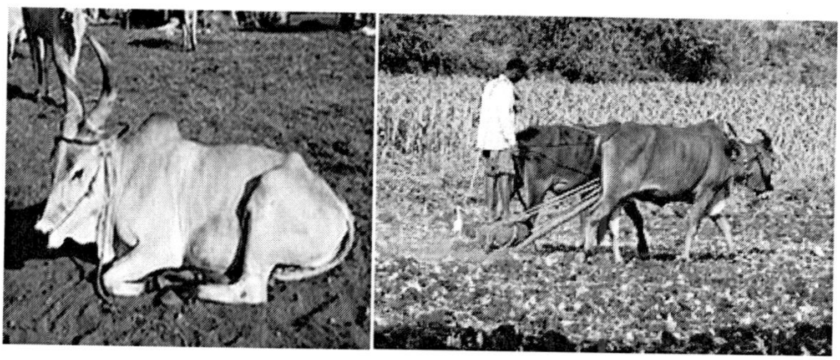

OX (Gaur-Bos frontali) IUCN: VU (Vulnerable)

Kingdom	:	Animalia
Phylum	:	Chordata
Class	:	Mammalia
Order	:	Artiodactyla
Family	:	Bovidae
Subfamily	:	Bovinae
Genus	:	Bos
Species	:	Bos *frontali*

Ecology

The animal weighs about a ton. The castrated males are used as draft animals and invariably white in colour but black and red colour ox are also found. They have been domesticated in about 4000 years B.C. almost in all states of India and they are very useful for Agriculture. An ox (plural oxen), is a bovine trained as a draft animal in Bihar and in all the states of India. Oxen are commonly castrated adult male cattle; and castration makes the animals easier to control. Oxen are used for plowing, for transport (pulling carts, hauling wagons) for threshing grain by trampling, and for powering machines that grind grain or supply irrigation. Oxen are usually yoked in pairs. They are popularly known as bullock.

Working oxen are taught to respond to the signals of *ox-driver or cart driver.* These signals are given by verbal command and body language, reinforced by a whip. In India, most cart drivers were known for their loud voices and forthright local language. Verbal commands for draft animals vary widely used throughout the world. Ox trainers favour larger animals for their ability to do more work. Oxen are therefore usually of larger breeds, and are usually males because they are generally larger. In western countries Oxen after use as draft animals are sacrificed for meat.

Chapter - 7

The State Animal of Chhatisgarh; Wild Water Buffalo

Wild Water Buffalo (Bubalus bubalus arnee): IUCN Category –EN (Endangered), India Schedule I

Kingdom	:	Animalia
Phylum	:	Chordata
Class	:	Mammalia
Order	:	Artiodactyla
Family	:	Bovidae
Genus	:	Bubalus
Species	:	*Bubalus bubalus arnee* (Kerr, 1792)

Body Structure

The *wild* water buffalo, Bubalus bubalus arnee, also called Asian buffalo, Asiatic buffalo. The wild water buffalo is one of the largest herbivore animal and measures about over 200 cm standing at the shoulders. They are also called Asiatic Buffalo. They have a black body but the toes are white. Both male and female wild water buffalo also bear two horns, which are flat and are curved to the top and widely spreading up to 2 m. They are larger and heavier than domestic buffalo, and weigh from 600 to 1,200 kg and their body length is 240 to 300 cm with a tail 60 to 100 cm long. The height at the shoulder is 150 to 190 cm. They have tuft of hair on the forehead, and the ears are comparatively small. The tip of the tail is bushy.

Ecology

The domestic buffalo have originated from them. A few DNA sequences are available from wild water buffalo populations. Wild populations are considered to be the progenitor of modern domesticated water buffalo, but the genetic variation within *B. arnee* is unclear. They can mate with domestic buffalo and produce fertile offspring. They possess excellent power of hearing, sight and scent.

They are found in Chhatisgarh, western part of Odisha, Madhya Pradesh, Assam and Arunachal Pradesh and south-east Asia. They graze in small groups and prefer to live in wet grasslands adjacent to forests. During day time they love to spend time in shallow water ponds.

The global population of water buffalo has been estimated at 4000 individuals, of which 3,300 to 3500 (90 per cent) live in India, mostly in Assam, mainly in Kaziranga National Park. A small population (1000-1500) *lives in Chhatisgarh,* western part of Odisha and in Madhya Pradesh.

Nepal's only population lives in the Koshi Tappu Wildlife Reserve. They have grown from 63 individuals in 1976 to 432 as per the latest census in 2016 with 120 males, 182 females and 130 calves. Since there are no Leopard, Tiger or Dhole in the reserve, the annual growth rate of wild buffalo is high. With an increase in the population, the authorities are considering a possible transfer of some individuals to the floodplains of Chitwan National Park in order to expand their numbers at other sites within Nepal. In and around Bhutan's Royal Manas National Park, a small number of wild water buffalo occur.

They are both diurnal and nocturnal. Adult females and their young form stable group of as many as 30 individuals. They have home ranges of 170 to 1,000 ha including areas for resting, grazing, wallowing and drinking. Groups are led by old cows, even when bulls accompany the group. Several groups form a herd of 30 to 500 animals that gather at resting areas. Adult males form bachelor groups of up to 10 individuals, with older males often being solitary, and spend the dry season apart from the females. They breed typically in October and November. However, some populations breed year round. Dominant males mate with the females of a group (clan) who subsequently drive them off. The gestation period is 10 to 11 months, with an inter-birth interval of one year. They usually give birth to a single offspring. Age at sexual maturity is 18 months for males, and three years for females. The maximum lifespan is 25 years in the wild.

Diet

They are grazers, feeding mainly on graminoids when available, such as Bermuda grass, and *Cyperus* sedges. They also eat other herbs, crops such as rice, sugarcane, jute. Fruits, and bark, as well as browsing on trees and shrubs.

Threats and Conservation

Tigers, and crocodiles are the main predators and they prey on adult wild water buffalo. Asian black bears have also been reported to predate on them.

The other threat for the reduction in population is: (i) interbreeding with domestic buffalo in and around protected areas, (ii) habitat loss of floodplain areas in Assam due to conversion to agriculture and hydropower development; (iii) degradation of wetlands due to invasive species such as stem twiners and lianas; (iv) diseases and parasites transmitted by domestic livestock; (v) Interspecific competition for food and water between wild buffalo and domestic stock. *Bubalus arnee* is included in CITES Appendix III, and is legally protected in India, Bhutan, India, Nepal, and Thailand.

Chapter - 8

The State Animal of Goa: Gaur (*Bos gaurus*)

The Indian Gaur (Bos gaurus), IUCN: EN (Endangered), India: Schedule I, Cites: I

Kingdom	:	Animalia
Phylum	:	Chordata
Class	:	Mammalia
Order	:	Artiodactyla
Family	:	Bovidae
Genus	:	*Bos*
Species	:	*Bos gaurus* Smith, 1827

The Sanskrit word *gaur-mriga* means a kind of buffalo. The gaur (*Bos gaurus*), is also called Indian bison. It is the native to the Indian Subcontinent and Southeast Asia. Its population declined considerably in parts of its range during the last few decades. It has been listed as Vulnerable on the IUCN Red List. However, the population is stable now in well-protected areas in India, and are rebuilding. The domesticated form of the Gaur is called *Gayal* (*Bos frontalis*) or *Mithun*. The Malayan gaur is called *seladang*, and the Burmese gaur is called *pyoung*.

Body Structure

The gaur is a strong and massively built species with a high convex ridge on the forehead between the horns, which bends forward, causing a deep hollow in the profile of the upper part of the head. There is a prominent ridge on the back. The ears are very large. The body colour of the adult gaur is dark brown or black. And the muzzle is pale coloured. The lower part of the legs is pure white or tan. The tail is shorter than in the typical oxen. They have a distinct ridge running from the shoulders to the middle of the back and the shoulders may be as much as 12 cm higher than the rump. The hair is short, fine and glossy, and the hooves are narrow and pointed.

The Gaur has a head-and-body length of 250 to 330 cm with a 70 to 105 cm long tail, and is 142 to 220 cm high at the shoulder, averaging about 188 cm in males and 168 cm in females. At the top of its muscular hump just behind its shoulder, an average adult male is just under 200 cm tall and the male's girth at its midsection (behind its shoulders) averages about 277 cm. Males are about one-fourth larger and heavier than females. Body weight can range widely from 588 to 1,500 kg in adult males and 440 to 1,000 kg in adult females. Body weights of Gaur in China and Malaysia are on average more than 20 per cent more massive than the gaurs of India.

Both sexes bear horns, which grow from the sides of the head, curving upwards. The horns are flattened at the base and curved throughout their length, and are bent inward and slightly backward at their tips. The colour of the horns is pale green or yellow throughout the greater part of their length, but the tips are black. The horns, of medium size by large bovid standards, grow to a length of 60 to 115 cm. In young animals the horns are smooth and polished. In old bulls they are rugged and dented at the base.

Ecology and behaviour

Two species that naturally co-exist with the Gaur are heavier: the Asian elephant (*Elephas maximus*) and Indian rhinoceros (*Rhinoceros unicornis*). Gaur habitat is characterised by large, relatively undisturbed forest tracts of evergreen or semi-evergreen and moist deciduous forests hilly terrain below an altitude of 1,500 to 1,800 m with availability of water, and an abundance of forage in the form of grasses, bamboo, shrubs, and trees…Low-lying areas seem to comprise optimal habitat.

The populations of Gaur in India, Bhutan and Bangladesh are estimated to comprise about 23,000 to 34,000 individuals. The Western Ghats and their adjacent hills in southern India constitute one of the most strongholds of gaur, in particular in the Wayanad – Nagarhole – Mudumalai – Bandipur complex..Major populations of about 2,000 individuals have been reported in both Nagarhole and Bandipur National Parks, over 1,000 individuals in Tadoba Andhari Tiger Project, 500–1000 individuals in both Periyar Tiger Reserve and Silent Valley and adjoining forest complexes, and over 800 individuals in Bhadra Wildlife Sanctuary. Besides, there few hundred individuals are located in Kaziranga Wildlife Sanctuary.

Gaur is basically diurnal. In some areas, they have become largely nocturnal due to forest loss. In central India, they are active at night, and are rarely seen in the open after 8 o'clock in the morning. During the dry season, herds congregate and remain in small areas, dispersing into the hills during the monsoon. Gaur drink water but they do not seem to bathe or wallow.

In January and February, Gaur lives in small herds of eight to 11 individuals, one of which is a bull. In April or May, more bulls join the herd for mating depending upon the number of mature females. Individual bulls may move from herd to herd, each mating with many cows. During the peak of the breeding season, unattached males to any herd wander widely in search of receptive females. After the mating season, adult bulls leave the herd and live alone or may form herds of bulls only. Herds wander 2–5 km each day for foraging. Sometimes herds may join in groups of 50 or more. Gaur herds are led by an old adult female, the matriarch. No serious fighting between males has been recorded, with size being the major factor in determining dominance. Males make a mating call of clear, resonant tones which is audible to about 2 km. Gaur has also been known to make a whistling snort as an alarm call, and a low, cow-like moo. The Gaur is very timid and shy animal despite their great size and power. When alarmed, gaur runs into the jungle at a surprising speed. However, in South India, where they are used to the presence of humans, they are said by local people to be very bold and aggressive. They graze alongside domestic cattle, sometimes killing them in fights. Gaur bulls may charge without provocation, especially during mating season, when the intense heat and parasitic insects make them more short-tempered than usual.

Diet

Long-term survival and conservation of these herbivores depend on the availability of preferred plant species for food. Wild gaur graze and browse on a wider variety of plants. They prefer the upper portions of plants, such as leaf blades, stems, flowers, seeds of grass species.They prefer to eat *Adina cordifolia* tree leaves. It is now known that 32 species of plants are utilised by them as food. They consume herbs, young shoots, flowers, fruits of elephant apple (*Dillenia* sp.) with a high preference for leaves. Food preference varies season wise. During monsoon and winter they graze on fresh grasses and herbs of legume family. They also browse on leaves of shrub species such as Strobilanthes callosus, Gardenia latifolia, and some other plants. They also feed on barks of teak (Tectona grandis), fruit of Cassia fistula and on the fruit and bark of cashew(Anacardium occidentale). Peak grazing activity occurs in the morning upto 8.30 am or 9 am and between 5.30 to 6.30 pm. During the day they rest under the shade of big trees with good canopy. High concentrations of calcium (22400 ppm) and phosphorus (400 ppm) have been reported in teak bark, so consumption of teak bark helps them to satisfy both mineral and other food needs. Understanding of their food habits and habitat requirement has conservation values.

Reproduction

Sexual maturity in Gaur occurs in second or third year after birth. The breeding season is from December to June but it can take place year-round. Females give birth to one calf (occasionally two) and the gestation period is about 275 days. Calves are weaned after seven to 12 months. The lifespan is about 30 years.

Threats and Conservation

Tigers and Crocodiles are the main natural predators of Gaur. Leopards and Dhole packs predate on unguarded calves or unhealthy gaur. Members of a gaur herd often form a circle surrounding the vulnerable calves and young ones, protecting them from predators.

Bos gaurus is listed in CITES Appendix I, and is legally protected in India. On 8 January 2001, the first cloned gaur was born at Trans Ova Genetics in Sioux Center, Iowa, USA. The calf was carried and brought successfully by a surrogate mother, a domestic cow (*Bos taurus*). While healthy at birth, the calf died within 48 hours due to common dysentery.

Chapter - 9

The State Animal of Gujarat: Asiatic Lion *(Panthera leo persica)*

Asiatic Lion **(Panthera leo persica)***-IUCN Category: EN (Endangered). India Schedule I, Cites:I*

Kingdom	:	Animalia
Phylum	:	Chordata
Class	:	Mammalia
Order	:	Carnivora
Family	:	Felidae
Genus	:	Panthera
Species	:	leo persica

Body Structure

The length of a full grown lion/lioness varies from 170 cm to

250 cm, with shoulder height of about 110 cm. An adult body weighs varies from 150 kg to 250 kg. The life span is about 20 years. The males possess beautiful mane. The females do not bear mane. They bear large paws tipped with sharp claws to grip prey and the claws are retractable. They have very strong hindlegs for fast running and pouncing on prey.

Ecology

Lions are large carnivores and fondly called the 'King of the Jungle'. Lions hunt from dusk to dawn and rest in the day. Lions are the true social cat. They live in groups, called 'Pride'. In one pride many female lioness, related to each other live along with their cubs. Male lions fight among themselves to remain in charge of the pride. The dominant male, who wins the race, becomes the sole owner of all lioness of the pride for mating. If the dominant male becomes physically weak, another strong male takes charge of the whole pride. The defeated male leaves the pride and lives alone or joins another pride if accepted. They usually hunt in groups and share the kill. A lion/lioness can run at 80 km per hour after the prey such as Deer, Cattle, and Pigs and other herbivores and jump over them and usually suffocating the prey by holding the neck and then they kill them. Normally Lioness run after the prey and kill the prey but all members of the pride share the food. Lions normally devour the meat and do not chew the bones, to which left over meat remain attached. Leopards, Jackles, Hyena and vultures eat the left over bones and attached rotten meat. One adult lion requires about twenty large mammals each year to survive.

Lions communicate between them by producing various sounds, but they are known for their roar. By roaring, they inform other pride members of their location and warn other males to keep away. A lion's roar can be heard several kilometers away. The pride usually goes to the water source for drinking together. Lions can remain many days without drinking water as they get the liquid from the blood of the prey.

Reproduction

There is no specific breeding time. If the female gets sexually heat, approaches the lion for mating and they remain together for some time in coitus. The gestation period is about 110 days and a female gives birth from one to six cubs. The average litter comprises three cubs. The cubs remain vulnerable to the attack of Hyenas, tigers etc. Lion cubs grow fast and become hunting worthy in one year and become sexually active within two to three years.

Threats and Conservation

Once upon a time, they were found in northen India but because of large scale poaching in the end of nineteenth century and uncontrolled shooting, diminishing habitat, especially savanna type vegetation (Bushes with grass and trees), reduction in prey population, human pressure etc. their population reached on the verge of extinction.

They are now confined to the Gir National Park in Gujarat. This could be possible because of the efforts of the Nawabs of Junagadh creating about 800 sq.km of wildlife sanctuary. Lions are now protected by law. About 300 of them live in Gir forest of Gujarat. Lions once lived in southern Europe, throughout Africa and parts of Asia. At present they are confined to African game reserves. The Asiatic lion is now confined to the Gir forest in Gujarat, India. Lion is the state animal of Gujarat.

Chapter - 10

The State Animal of Himachal Pradesh: Snow Leopard (*Uncia uncia or Panthera uncia*), India: Schedule I

Snow Leopard (wikipedia)

Kingdom	:	Animalia
Phylum	:	Chordata
Class	:	Mammalia
Order	:	Carnivora
Family	:	Felidae
Genus	:	Uncia (= Panthera)
Species	:	Uncia (=Panthera) uncia

Snow Leopard (*Uncia uncia or Panthera uncia* (Schreber)-Indian Schedule-I, IUCN- EN(Endangered), IUCN-2017 VU.

The snow leopard (*Uncia uncia*) is a large cat native to the mountain ranges of Central and South Asia. Two subspecies have been recognised, but genetic differences between the two have not been clearly established. Both the Latinised genus name, *Uncia*, and English name *ounce* are derived from the Old French *once*, originally used for the European lynx.

Body Structure

On the average the length of the animal is 100 – 110 cm with a long tail measuring at 80 to 100 cm, longer than most of the cats. Snow leopards are slightly smaller than the other big cats (Panthera tigris) but, like them, body sizes vary, generally weighing between 27 and 55 kg, with an occasional large male reaching 75 kg and small female of under 25 kg. The average body weight is about 36 kg. They have a relatively short body, measuring in length from the head to the base of the tail 75 to 150 cm. They are stocky and shortlegged, standing about 60 at the shoulder. They have long, thick fur, and its colour varies from smoky gray to yellowish tan, with whitish underparts. Dark grey to black open rosettes on their bodies, with small spots of the same colour on their heads and larger spots on their legs and tails are found. Their eyes are pale green (unlike other cats) or grey in colour. The snow leopard cannot roar due to absence of larynx and therefore the vocalisation includes hisses, mews, growls and wailing.

Ecology

Snow leopards inhabit alpine and subalpine zones at elevations from 3,000 to 4,500 m. In the northern range countries, they also occur at lower elevations. The snow leopard is found in Himalayas between about 2000 m (in winter) and about 5000 m in summer. They are found in high altitudes of Arunachal Pradesh, Jammu and Kashmir, Sikkim, and Himachal Pradesh. Global warming and climate change has caused the tree line to be increased in altitude in Ladakh, resulting in the decrease of wild prey that depend on the plants for food and also affecting the distribution of snow leopard.

The size of the global wild population was estimated at 4,080–6,590 adults. Fewer than 2,500 individuals is estimated to be reproducing in the wild. As of 2016, estimates for the size of the global population vary from at least 4,080 to about 8,700 individuals.

The male snow leopard is solitary. The females live with cubs. They rear them in dens in the mountains for extended periods. An individual snow leopard lives within a well-defined home range, but usually does not defend its territory aggressively when encroached upon by other snow leopards.

Snow leopards use scent marks to indicate their territories. These are produced by scraping the ground with the hind feet and depositing urine or scat, and they spray urine onto rock.

Diet

Snow leopards are predators and actively hunt their prey. They eat whatever meat they can find. They can predate on animals two to four times their own weight, such as Himalayan tahr, horse, domestic cattle and camel and bharals (Himalayan blue sheep. They also eat rabbits, birds etc.

Reproduction

Snow leopards mate in winter. Paired snow leopards mate in the usual felid posture and copulation occurs from 12 to 36 times a day. Females have a gestation period of 90–100 days and the cubs are born between April and June. Oestrus typically lasts from five to eight days. After mating, males usually do not mate with another female. The mother gives birth in a rocky den or crevice lined with fur shed from her underside. Average litter size is about two and the range is one to five cubs. Although born with a thick coat of fur, the cubs are blind and helpless at birth, and weigh from 320 to 567 g. Their eyes open at around seven days. The cubs can walk at five weeks and are weaned by 10 weeks. When cubs are born, they have full black spots which turn into rosettes as the cubs grow to adolescence and to adult. The cubs leave the den when they are about two to four months old, and they remain with their mother until the cubs become independent after around 18–22 months. When they become about two years old, they may disperse even crossing wide expanses of flat terrain to seek out new hunting grounds. This likely helps reduce the inbreeding that would otherwise be common in their relatively isolated environments. Snow leopards become sexually mature at two to three years. The life span is around 15–18 years. In captivity they live for up to 25 years.

Threats and Conservation

They are heavily poached by human beings because of the beautiful thick and whitish, patterned with dark rosettes and spots fur.

The population of this beautiful leopard has declined to about one thousand animals in India and therefore they are now taken as protected animals under Schedule I. In a recent census (2017), their population has increased to about 4,000 in the world and IUCN has removed them from endangered category to vulnerable category (TOI, 2017). Threats include mining and other infrastructure development that affects their natural habitat. They are poached because of their beautiful fur. Hence they require protection measures.

Global Snow Leopard and Eco-system Protection Programme (GSLEP) is a joint initiative of range country governments, international agencies, civil society, and the private sector. Its goal is to secure the long-term survival of the snow leopard in its natural ecosystem.

At the GSLF meeting, the 12 range countries signed the Bishkek Declaration that "the snow leopard is an irreplaceable symbol of nations' natural and cultural heritage and an indicator of the health and sustainability of mountain ecosystems. Member countries recognise that mountain ecosystems inhabited by snow leopards provide essential ecosystem services, including storing and releasing water from the origins of river systems benefitting one-third of the world's human population; sustaining the pastoral and agricultural livelihoods of local communities which depend on biodiversity for food, fuel, fodder, and medicine; and offering inspiration, recreation, and economic opportunities."

Chapter - 11

The State Animal of Jammu and Kashmir: Kashmir Stag/Hanglu: Cervus elephas hanglu (Wagner), India: Schedule I

Kingdom	:	Animalia
Phylum	:	Chordata
Class	:	Mammalia
Order	:	Artiodactyla
Family	:	Bovidae
Subfamily	:	Antilopinae
Genus	:	Antilope(=Cervus) Pallas, 1766
Genus	:	Cervus
Species	:	Cervus elephas hanglu, IUCN: LC (Least Concerned), India: Schedule I

Cervus Elephas hanglu

There are nine species of deer found in India. They are (i) the Kashmir Stag (*Cervus elaphus hanglu*), (ii) Brow Antlered Deer, (*Cervus eldi eldi*), (iii) Sambar (*Cervus unicolor*), (iv) Barasingha or Swamp Deer (*Cervus duvauceli*), (v) Hog Deer (*Axis porcinus),* (vi) Spotted Deer or Chital (*Axis axis*), (vii) Muntjac or Barking Deer (*Muntiacus muntjak*), (viii) Musk Deer (Moschus moschiferus), (ix) Mouse Deer or Indian Chevrotain (*Tragulus meminna*).

Body Structure

The body colour of this deer is brown to light brown but the area under the tail is white. The ear and lips of this deer is also white in colour. Its horn usually have five or six times. The Kashmir Stag has a light rump patch in the body. The inner sides of the buttocks of Kashmir Stag are greyish white. The beam is strongly curved inward.

Ecology

Kashmir Stag or Hanglu is a big and beautiful herbivore. They live in group of two to eighteen animals in jungles adjacent to rivers and water sources. They are found in Kashmir and Himachal Pradesh in about 3000 m to 10,000 m altitude. At present they are mainly found in Dhachigam National Park area of Kashmir. In summer they come down to lower altitudes in groups for food and water.

Threats and conservation

These deers was threatened due to its habitat destruction, over-grazing by domestic livestock, and poaching by human beings.

It is estimated that there were about 5000 individuals in the beginning of twentieth century and their population dwindled to about 150 individuals by 1970. In the meantime, because of the protective action taken by the project Hangul of the state government of Jammu & Kashmir, with the assistance of IUCN and the WWF, the population is showing increasing trend. And the population has increased to over 340 by 1980. There are plans to breed them in captivity to increase their population and chances of survival.

Chapter - 12

The State Animal of Jharkhand, Karnataka and Kerala: Indian Elephant: *Elephas maximus indicus*

Elephas maximus indicus

IUCN Category: Endangered, India: Schedule 1, Cites: I

Kingdom	:	Animalia
Phylum	:	Chordata
Class	:	Mammalia
Order	:	Proboscidea
Family	:	Elephantidae
Genus	:	Elephas
Species	:	maximus indicus

Body Structure

Elephant is the largest land animal. Its height is about 305 cm at shoulder. The body weight is about four to five tons. The huge body of an adult elephant bears four very strong legs, a tail and a proboscis which touches the ground and a pair large size ears. The male elephants bear a pair of tusks; each of the tusks may measure on the average 137 cm. Elephants use their proboscis for collection of feed material and water and then put the materials into mouth. The proboscis can be moved up and down, laterally and therefore it is used for collection of leaves, twigs etc for food. It is muscular and very strong and the proboscis is also used to defend the animal from the predators such as tigers. In the front of the proboscis, a scent gland lies in the form of a pouch. The pouch helps the animal to smell the materials and the air around. Therefore, the proboscis always remains moving.

Ecology

Elephants live in groups. They move from place to place in a line and the oldest female takes the lead or manage the herd about twelve or more animals in the group. Although declared *as the state animal of Jharkhand, Karnataka and Kerala*, but they are found in forests of Andhra Pradesh, Odisha, Jharkhand, Bihar, Karnataka, Kerala, Tamil Nadu, West Bengal, Uttar Pradesh and North-eastern states.

The elephant is associated with cultural functions in India and they have lent majesty in royal processions and in religious festivals. They are used for forestry operations and to carry logs to the desired destinations. Elephants are also used to carry people to the jungle for hunting of carnivores and for tourist safaris. Elephants are intelligent animals and trained by human beings to do lot of their work. As the Hindu god 'Sri Ganesh' bears head like a baby elephant, the animal is revered in India. In India, they are now protected animals by law. Elephants are also found in South-East Asia and in Africa. The African elephant is larger in size.

Diet

They are herbivores and eat huge amount of vegetation. They require a large area for movement in the forest or from one forest range to another forest.

They are herbivores and feed on woody plants, twigs and leaves, grass, bamboo, palm and all eatable fruits. An adult requires about 300 kg of plant material as food every day and about 230 litres of water to drink every day.

Reproduction

In some specific time of the year, the males remain sexually excited.This is called 'Musth'. During 'musth' period, the ophthalmic gland situated near the eyelid secretes a liquid with deep smell. Normally, the males mate with the females during 'musth' period. It is also known the elephants can enter into coitus any time of the year. At the time of birth a baby elephant may weigh 100 kg and its height is about 1 metre and its body contains hairs. The gestation period is 21 months and the female delivers one baby elephant. At the time of delivery, other adult female assist in the delivery process. The life span of the Indian elephant is about 70 to 80 years.

Threats and Conservation

Because of the huge reduction of forest cover, they very often visit crop fields and human settlements in search of food. In view of this there is now Human-Elephant conflict, which causes death of elephants and human beings. The male elephant tusks are source of ivory and therefore, they are illegally poached by some people. The other threat is high voltage electric line passing through forests and often charged wires hang upto lower heights and elephants become victim. Another important threat is poaching for tusks, which fetch high value in forest market.

They are classified by *IUCN Category: Endangered, and India-Schedule 1.*

Project Elephant was launched by the Government of India in the year 1992 as a Centrally Sponsored Scheme with following objectives:

1. To protect elephants, their habitat and corridors,
2. To address issues of man-animal conflict,
3. Welfare of captive elephants.

The Project is being mainly implemented in 16 States / UTs, viz. Andhra Pradesh, Arunachal Pradesh, Assam, Chhattisgarh, Jharkhand, Karnataka, Kerala, Maharashtra, Meghalaya, Nagaland, Odisha, Tamil Nadu, Tripura, Uttarakhand, Uttar Pradesh, West Bengal.

Government of India and different state governments have established protected areas for them. The following table gives the elephant population in different protected areas in different state.

Sl. No.	*States*	*Elephant Population*	
		2007	*2012*
1	Arunachal Pradesh	1690	1690*
2	Assam	5281	5281*
3	Meghalaya	1811	1811*
4	Nagaland	152	212
5	Tripura	59	59*
6	West Bengal	325-350	325-350*
7	Jharkhand	624	688
8	Odisha	1862	1930
9	Chattisgarh	122	215
10	Uttarakhand	1346	1346*
11	Uttar Pradesh	380	380
12	Tamil Nadu	3867	3726
13	Karnataka	4035	3900-7458**
14	Kerela	6068	6177
15	Andhra Pradesh	28	41
16	Maharashtra	7	4
		27657-27682	**27785-31368**

Chapter - 13

The State Animal of Madhya Pradesh, and Uttar Pradesh: *Barasingha (Swamp Deer)*: *Cervus duvaucelii* (G.Cuvier)

Barasingha (Cervus (=Rucervus) duvaucelii), IUCN: VU (Vulnerable), India: Schedule I.

Kingdom	:	Animalia
Phylum	:	Chordata
Class	:	Mammalia
Order	:	Artiodactyla
Family	:	Cervidae
Genus	:	*Rucervus (Cervidae)*
Species	:	*R. duvaucelii*

Body Structure

Barasingha Deer is known for its big horns and beautiful brown colour body. The deer stands about 135 cm at the shoulder and it is called Barasingha as 12 points are present on its horn. The horns are branched and body contains soft hair. The body colour changes in different seasons i.e. in summer it looks little grayish dull. The horns are shed periodically in young ones and new horns emerge. Horn shedding usually occurs during the breeding season. The sense of smell is very strong in this deer.

Ecology

Barasingha live in very large groups. Herds of 50 animals are common and sometimes hundred of animals are found in one group. Groups of males and groups of females are found separately.

Diet

They feed on grass and other vegetation and distributed in grasslands of Madhya Pradesh, Uttar Pradesh, and Assam. There are two recognised races of this deer. One race lives on land and the other race prefers swamps.

Reproduction

During the breeding season they join together for mating and the get separated. The young ones live with their mothers in the group. The group is lead by a strong adult.

Threats and Conservation

The predators are the tigers, leopards, Hyena, Jackal and other predators. They are poached by human beings for meat, skin and horns. Conservation measures have been taken keeping them in protected areas and poaching has been declared illegal.

Chapter - 14

The State Animal of Maharashtra: Indian Giant Squirrel: Ratufa indica

Ratufa indica IUCN: VU (Vulnerable), India: Schedule: II, Cites: Appendix II

Kingdom	:	Animalia
Phylum	:	Chordata
Class	:	Mammalia
Genus	:	Ratufa
Species	:	indica

Body Structure

Ratufa indica, native to India, is the giant squirrels with about 40 cm long body with a bushy tail of about 60 cm long. On the average an adult weighs 2 kg.

Ecology

These squirrels are exclusively forest arboreal rodents. The Indian giant squirrel is an upper-canopy dwelling species, which requires "tall profusely branched trees for the construction nests. They are diurnal. They are also called Malabar giant squirrels with dark reddish brown body and look gorgeous. They are found in deciduous and mixed evergreen forests of peninsular India. The species is endemic to India. They rarely come to the ground and move from tree to tree leaping through branches. They can jump up to 6 m (20 ft) from tree to tree. Few subspecies of Ratufa India have been recognised (Table1) and they are (i) Ratufa indica indica, (found in Mumbai region and most of the places in India), (ii) Ratufa indica centralis, (found mainly in central India), (iii) Ratufa indica dealbata (mainly found in Surat, Gujarat area), (iv) Ratufa indica maxima (found in Malabar region, Odisha, West Bengal- synonym to Ratufa indica bengalensis). The four subspecies vary in their body colour. They are believed to play important role in seed dispersal and thus protecting the ecosystem.

***Ratufa indica* subspecies, names of Authority and Synonym**

Subspecies	*Authority and year*	*Synonyms*
Ratufa indica indica	Erxleben (1777)	*bombaya, elphinstoni, purpureus,* superans
R. i. centralis	Ryley (1913)	none
R. i. dealbata	Blanford (1897)	none
R. i. maxima	Schreber (1784)	*bengalensis, malabarica*

Nest Building

The Indian Giant Squirrel lives alone or in pairs *and come together for breeding*. They build large globular nests of twigs and leaves, placing them on thinner branches where large predators cann't get to them. These nests become conspicuous in deciduous forests during the dry season. An individual may build several nests in a small area of forest which are used as sleeping quarters, with one being used as a nursery. *The giant squirrels produce a characteristic* staccato call. These squirrels are found in forests of Maharashtra and also commonly found in Similipal Biosphere in Odisha. A sanctuary to protect the squirrels has been established at Srivilliputhur in Tamil Nadu.

Diet

They are largely herbivores and eat any edible vegetable matter namely, fruits, nuts, shoots, buds, bark, and tender leaves and also occasionally eat insects and their larvae and bird eggs. Their incisor teeth are very strong and the teeth perhaps grow throughout the life.

Reproduction

The female may mate with more than one male. The gestation period is *six to seven weeks and two or three young ones are born*. Captive breeding has indicated births of young ones in March, April, September and December. The young weigh about 74 g at birth and have a length of about 27 cm.

Threats and Conservation

Birds of prey and leopards predate on them. They are the natural predators. When in danger, instead of jumping from tree to tree, they try to hide from the predator by lying flat on the tree trunk or hiding in tree trunk cavity if any.

IUCN: VU (Vulnerable)

Chapter - 15

The State Animal of Manipur: Brow-antlered Deer (Sangai): (Cervus eldi eldi)

Sangai male and female

Sangai male with a fawn

Sangai (*Cervus eldi eldi*) IUCN Category: (CR)-(Critically Endangered), India: Schedule: I, Cites: I

Kingdom	:	Animalia
Phylum	:	Chordata
Class	:	Mammalia
Order	:	Artiodactyla
Family	:	Cervidae
Genus	:	*Rucervus (= Cervus)*
Species	:	*Cervus (=Rucervus) eldii*
Subspecies	:	*Cervus eldii eldii*

This deer is endemic to Manipur and endangered. The common name is Sangai. The name sangai (*sa* "animal" and *ngai* "in awaiting") was coined from its peculiar posture and behaviour while running. By nature, the deer, particularly the males, even when running for its life stops occasionally and looks back as if he is waiting for someone and hence the name. Its common English name is Manipur brow-antlered deer.

Body Structure

The brow-antlered deer is a medium-sized deer, having with height and weight of a fully grown stag around 115–125 cm at shoulder and 95 to 110 kg body weight respectively and with distinctive antlers, measuring 100–120 cm. in length with very long brow line, which form the main beam. The two tines form a continuous curve at right angles to the closely set pedicels. This signifies its name, brow-antlered deer. The forward protruding beam appears to come out from the eyebrow. The antlers of the opposite sides are unsymmetrical with respect to each other. The beams are unbranched initially whereas curvature increases as length increases and they get forked also.

The sexes are dimorphic in body size and weight. The height and weight of the female are shorter and less as compared to the males. The length of the body from the base to the ear up to the tail is about 145 to 155 cm in both sexes. The tail is short and rump patch is not pronounced.

Ecology

The brow-antlered deer is found in its natural habitat only at Keibul Lamjao National Park over the floating biomass locally called "phumdi" in the south-eastern part of Loktak Lake. The park covers an area of 40 km^2 and the home range of the deer in the park is confined to 15–20 km^2.

Manipur Cultural Symbol

There are number of folklores in Manipur based on Sangai. One of the folklore is based on a legendary hero Kadeng Thangjahanba of Moirang once captured a pregnant sangai from Torbung Lamjao for a gift to his beloved Tonu Laijinglembi during an animal hunting expedition. On his return from the hunting expedition, as fate would have it, he found his beloved married to the king. The heartbroken hero released the gravid deer free in the wild of Keibul Lamjao. Since then the place became the home of sangai. In folklore of Manipur, a prince called Pudangkoi of Luwang clan had, by the grace of a divine entity, transformed himself into a deer which has later on called sangai. Further, there were references of sangai head with crown of antlers, being decorated on the head of royal boat called Hiyang Hiren. Manipuri's folklore based on a popular folk legend, the sangai is interpreted as the connecting soul between humans and the nature. The slaying of the sangai is considered an unpardonable sin as it breaks up of the cordial relationship between humans and the nature. When humans love and respect the sangai, it is respecting nature. In the sangai, therefore, humans find a way of expressing their love for the nature. Socially, in Manipur, the sangai is the symbol of a prised possession of the state. The sangai is, therefore the apple of the eye for the people.

Food

Phumdi is the important and unique part of the lake. It is the floating biomass of entangled aquatic vegetation formed by the accumulation of organic debris and biomass with soil. The thickness of Phumdi varies from few centimeters to two meters and it floats with 80 per cent under water. The humus of phumdi is black in colour and very spongy with large number of pores. Sangai feed on a variety of water living plants, grasses, herbaceous plants, and shoots. *Zizania latifolia*, *Saccharum munja*, *S. bengalensis*, *Erianthus procerus*, *E. ravernnae*, etc.

Feeding behaviour of sangai exhibits a bimodal activity patterns as they graze usually early morning approximately 4:30 am and generally continue up to 8:00 am. On cloudy morning the period may extend to 10:00 am. In the evening it starts at 3:00 pm and continue up to 6:00 pm. After feeding it takes rest under thick and tall reeds and grasses. At night some of them even rest on the hillocks.

Reproduction

Rutting takes place in between February and May. Males compete with each other to gain control of a harem of females to mate with them. Gestation period is 220 to 240 days and normally a single calf is born. The young are spotted at birth; these spots fade as the animal grows. The young are weaned at seven months of age, and becomes sexually mature from 18 months of age. The sangai has a maximum lifespan of around 10 years in the wild.

Threats and Conservation

The sangai faces a two-pronged danger to its life. Firstly, its habitat is steadily degenerating by reason of continuous inundation and flooding by high water caused as the result of artificial reservoir of the National Hydroelectric Power Corporation Loktak. Secondly, poachers are out there to trap and slay the deer at the slightest opportunity.

The number of deer listed in the IUCN Red Data Book was only 14 in 1975. In 1990s, there were only 100 of them. In Manipur they are called Sangai. After the declaration of the area as a national park and with strict conservation measures taken up by the Forest Department, the fear of its extinction has been greatly reduced. There are now few hundred of them in wild. The sangai was believed to be almost extinct by 1950. Since then, the State Government has taken positive measures for the protection of this rare and endangered species. The number of endangered deer sangai found in Manipur has increased from 204 in 2013 to 260, according to the latest census conducted in March 2016 jointly by Wildfire Wing, Forest department, State government, Manipur University and Wildfire Institute of India.

In 1983, the 103 megawatt capacity National Hydroelectric Power Corporation Loktak was commissioned with the objective of ensuring rapid development in the State. A maximum high water level of 168.5 meters above mean sea level (MSL) is maintained in the Loktak Lake to feed the reservoir for the hydel project. This high water level had wreaked havoc in the Keibul Lamjao National Park. The high water level, maintained continuously through the year, had disturbed the natural life cycle of the vegetation growth, the phumdi, upon which the sangai thrives. The deer feed on several types of vegetation that grow on the phumdi. The vegetation also provides shelter to the deer and other wildlife in the park.The life-cycle of the phumdi involves floating on the water surface during season of high water as in the monsoons. In the lean season, when the water level reduces, the biomass comes into contact with the lake bed and the deers secure the required nutrient from there. When the rains come again and they become afloat, the biomass have enough 'food'—the nutrients—stored in their roots and their life continues. What is happening now, according to local scientists who are studying the phenomena, is that with continuous high water in the lake throughout the year much of this process of 'feeding' on the nutrient in the lakebed had discontinued. The result is that the biomass are losing weight and getting thinner by the year. This is a bad sign for the sangai habitat. There are reports of local people cutting up the phumdi into sizable pieces and then towing away these with dugout canoe for 'selling' to fish culture owners. This is another potential danger to the sangai habitat. It meant humans are now aiding the process of annihilating the habitat area, supplementing to the rapid degeneration of the habitat. Alternative methods are to be found to save sangai. (wikipedia).

Chapter - 16

The State Animal of Meghalaya: Clouded Leopard (Neofelis nebulosa)

Clouded Leopard (Neofelis nebulosa), IUCN Category: VU (Vulnerable), India: Schedule I, Cites: I

Kingdom	:	Animalia
Phylum	:	Chordata
Class	:	Mammalia
Order	:	Carnivora
Family	:	Felidae
Genus	:	*Neofelis*
Species	:	Neofelis nebulosa (Griffith, 1821)

The scientific name of the genus *Neofelis* is a composite of the Greek word-meaning “new”, and the Latin word *feles* meaning “cat”, so it literally means “new cat”.

Body Structure

The body weight of clouded leopard varies between 11.5 and 23 kg. Females vary in head-to-body length from 68.6 to 94 cm with a tail of 61 to 82 cm long. Males are larger at 81 to 108 cm with a tail 74 to 91 cm long. Their height at shoulder varies from 50 to 55 cm. They have exceptionally long, about 4 cm or longer piercing canine teeth, the upper being about three times as long as the basal width of the socket. They have the largest canines in proportion to their body size, matching the tiger in canine length and therefore, they are often referred to as a “modern-day sabre-tooth.” The first premolar is usually absent, and they also have a very distinct long and slim skull with well-developed occipital and sagittal crests to support the enlarged jaw muscles.

The Clouded Leopard is a strong animal, measuring about 195 cm in length and weighs upto 30 kg. They are an enigmatic animal found in tropical and subtropical dense evergreen forests. The body colour varies from grey to yellowish-brown and the face of the leopard is marked with cheek stripes. Dark blotches are found in its flanks. The fur of clouded leopards is of a dark grey often largely obliterated by black and dark dusky-grey blotched pattern. There are black spots on the head, and the ears are black. Partly fused or brokenup stripes run throughout the body. Two large blotches of dark dusky-grey hair on the side of the shoulders are each emphasised posteriorly by a dark stripe, which passes on to the foreleg and breaks up into irregular spots. The flanks are marked by dark dusky-grey irregular blotches bordered behind by long, oblique, irregularly curved or looped stripes. These blotches yielding the clouded pattern suggest the name of the cat. The underparts and legs are spotted, and the tail is marked by large, irregular, paired spots. Females are slightly smaller than males. Their eye colour are usually either greyish-green or brownish yellow in colour. Their legs are short and stout, with broad paws. They have rather short limbs compared to the other big cats, but their hind limbs are longer than their front limbs to allow for increased jumping and leaping capabilities.

Their ulnae and radii are not fused, which also contributes to a greater range of motion when climbing trees and stalking prey.

Ecology

The leopard is largely arboreal and nocturnal. In India, Clouded leopards occur in Assam, northern West Bengal, Sikkim, Arunachal Pradesh, Manipur, Meghalaya, Mizoram, Nagaland, and Tripura. In the Himalayas, they were found at altitudes of 2,500–3,720 m between April 2008 and May 2010 in the Khangchendzonga Biosphere Reserve, Sikkim.

They occur from the Himalayan foothills in Nepal and India to Myanmar, Bhutan, Thailand, Peninsular Malaysia, Indochina, and in China south of the Yangtze River. In 2009, a few clouded leopards were sighted in the Chittagong Hill Tracts of Bangladesh.

Clouded leopards are excellent climbers among the cats. In captivity, they have been observed to climb down vertical tree trunks head first, and hang on to branches with their hind paws bent around tree branches. They can easily jump up to 4 feet high.

They were thought to be nocturnal predators of dense primary forest. They also use trees as daytime rest sites, but also spend a significant proportion of time on the ground. Some daytime movement has been observed depending on their prey and the level of human disturbance, suggesting they are not strictly nocturnal. Their low densities, and because they inhabit densely forests or vegetated habitats makes the counting and monitoring of clouded leopards difficult. Much is not known of their natural history and behaviour in the wild. However, their behaviour has been observed in captivity in zoological gardens. Clouded leopards have been observed to mark their territory by scent mark in captivity by urine-spraying and head-rubbing on prominent objects, although the size of their home ranges is unknown. They have a wide range of vocalisations, including mewing, hissing, growling, moaning, and snorting. When communicating, two individuals will emit low snorting sounds that are called prusten when approaching each other in a friendly manner. They also use long-call communication for distances, which could either be a type of mating call between different territories or a warning call to other cats encroaching on other territories. They live a solitary lifestyle.

Diet

Its food is herbivores, mainly deer and rabbit. When hunting, clouded leopards either come down from the trees and stalk their prey or hide in the bush and wait for the prey to come nearby. After making a kill and eating, they usually retreat to the trees sometime carrying part of the body part of the prey. Their prey includes both arboreal and terrestrial vertebrates. The prey species include hog deer, slow loris, porcupine, and squirrel. Known prey species in China include barking deer and pheasants.

From studies in Thailand protected areas using radio collared method is known that Home ranges of two females were 25.7 km^2 and 22.9 km^2, and of two males were 29.7 km^2) and 49.1 km^2.

Reproduction and Life Span

First reproduction occurs when males and females average 26 months. Mating usually occurs during December and March. It has been reported that the males tend to be very aggressive during mating. Males, known to bite the female on the neck during courtship, sometimes severing her cervical vertebrae. Male and female meet and mate multiple times over the course of several days. The male rides over the female and grasps the neck. The female responds favourably with vocalisation that encourages the male to continue the coitus. After copulation, the male then leaves the spot and is not involved in raising the cubs. On the average estrus lasts six days, estrous cycle averages 30 days. The gestation period varies between 87 to 99 days. Females give birth to a litter of one to five (common three) cubs. They rear their cubs in hollows of trees.

Initially, the young are blind and helpless, much like the young of many other cats, and weigh from 140 to 280 g). The young can see within 10 days of birth, and become active within five weeks, and are fully weaned at around three months of age. The cubs attain the adult coat pattern at around six months. Probably they become independent after around 10 months. Females are able to bear one litter each year.

The mother is believed to hide her cubs in dense vegetation while she goes to hunt. In captivity, they have an average lifespan of 11 years. One individual has lived to be almost 17 years old.

Threats and Conservation

One of the main threats to clouded leopard is Poaching for illegal trade of skin. Habitat loss due to deforestation is another important threat and many of the remaining habitats-forest areas are too small to ensure the long-term persistence of clouded leopard populations. In Myanmar, 301 body parts of at least 279 clouded leopards, mostly skins and skeletons, were on sale in four markets, surveyed between 1991 and 2006. These markets cater to international buyers, although clouded leopards are completely protected under Myanmar's national legislation.

Neofelis nebulosa is listed in CITES Appendix I and protected over most of its range. Hunting is banned in India, Bangladesh, China, Malaysia, Myanmar, Nepal, Taiwan, Thailand, and Vietnam. These bans, however, are poorly enforced in India, and some other countries. It is in IUCN vulnerable list. As of December 2011, 222 clouded leopards are believed to exist in zoos. Captive breeding programme is being tried in few Zoos.

Chapter - 17

The State Animal of Mizoram: Himalayan Serow: (*Capricornis thar*)

Himalayan Serow: (**Capricornis thar*****), IUCN: NT (near threatened), listed in CITES Appendix I***

Kingdom	:	Animalia
Phylum	:	Chordata
Class	:	Mammalia
Order	:	Artiodactyla
Family	:	Bovidae
Genus	:	*Capricornis*
Species	:	Capricornis thar Hodgson 1831

The Himalayan serow (Capricornis thar) is a mountain goat native to the eastern Himalayas and popularly known as goat-antelope.

Body Structure

The Serow has a large head, donkey like ears, thick neck and short limbs. They are medium-sized goat-like or antelope-like.

Ecology

They are distributed mainly in Eastern Himalayas in high altitudes. They also occur in east and southeast Bangladesh, Bhutan, Nepal, northern India including Sikkim. One study has estimated the presence of 1.6 serow/km^2.

Diet

They graze in green meadow in Himalayas in India.

Threats and Conservation

The species is listed as Near Threatened on the IUCN Red List because the population is considered to be declining due to habitat loss and poaching for its meat.

Pangolakha Wildlife Sanctuary in East Sikkim is now the main protected abode of Serows. Kedarnath Wildlife Sanctuary (Uttarankhand) also houses the Serows. It was earlier named as the national mammal of Sikkim.

Chapter - 18

The State Animal of Odisha: Sambar (*Rusa (=Cervus) unicolor*)

Rusa (=Cervus) unicolor), IUCN Category: VU (Vulnerable), India: Schedule III

Kingdom	:	Animalia
Phylum	:	Chordata
Class	:	Mammalia
Order	:	Artiodactyla
Family	:	Cervidae

Genus	:	*Rusa* (=Cervus)
Species	:	Rusa (=Cervus) *unicolor*

Sambar is the largest Indian Deer, native to Indian subcontinent, south-east Asia and southern part of China. At present seven subspecies of sambar are recognised. The appearance and the size of sambar vary widely. This has led to taxonomic confusion in the past; over 40 different scientific synonyms have been used for the species. The name "sambar" is also used to refer to the Philippine deer, called the "Philippine sambar" and the Javan rusa, called the "Sunda sambar".

Body Structure

In general, they attain a height of 102 to 160 cm at the shoulder and may weigh as much as 546 kg, though more typically 220 to 350 kg. Head and body length varies from 1.62 to 2.7 m, with a 22 to 35 cm tail. Females are smaller than males. The coat is coarse and dark and can be yellowish-brown to dark grey in colour and usually forms a ruff around the throat. They bear a red sore patch, especially in adult males and pregnant or lactating females in the neck region and the function of this patch is not known. This red sore patch sometimes oozes a white liquid, and is apparently glandular in nature.

The brow tines being simple and the beams forked at the tip, so they have only three times in the horn. The antlers are up to 110 cm long in fully adult individuals. Only the males have antlers. Sambar also has a small but dense mane, and the mane is more prominent in males. It has a long tail uncharacteristic of a deer, and is generally black above with a whitish underside.

Ecology and Behaviour

They are found in the mountain forests in northen and south-eastern part of India, especially in Odisha and nearby places. The sambar is also distributed in much of Southeast Asia as far north as the south-facing slopes of the Himalayas. In the Himalayan foothills, and Myanmar, Sambar ranges up to an altitude of 3,500 m. They are found in Burma, Thailand, Indochina, the Malay Peninsula, South China and in the Indonesian islands of Sumatra and Borneo. It inhabits in variety of forests namely, tropical dry forests, tropical seasonal forests, subtropical mixed wood forests with stands of conifers, broadleaved deciduous and broadleaved evergreen trees, to tropical rainforests, with dense cover of deciduous shrubs and grasses, and close to the water sources.

Sambar is nocturnal or crepuscular. The size of the home range are probably equally variable, but have been recorded as 1,500 ha for males and 300 ha for females in India. The females live in small herds of up to 16 individuals. In some areas, the average herd consists of only three or four individuals, consisting of an adult female, her most recent young, and perhaps a subordinate, immature female. This is different pattern from other deer species, which usually live in larger groups. The males are solitary except the breeding season. All adults can scream or make short, high-pitched sounds when alarmed. Sambars congregate near water source and are good swimmers. They more commonly communicate with members of the group by scent marking and foot stamping. Stags wallow and dig their antlers in urine-soaked soil, and then rub against tree trunks. A stag also marks himself by spraying urine on his own face with a highly mobile penis.

Diet

Sambar feed on a wide variety of vegetation, including grasses, foliage, and browse, fruit, and water plants, depending on the availability and they also consume a variety of shrubs and trees. Sambar is capable of bipedalism for foraging, and stags stand and mark tree branches above them with their antlers. It has been observed that Sambar congregates in large herds in protected areas such as national parks and reserves in India, Sri Lanka, and Thailand. They normally shed their antlers annually in April and May. In Taiwan, sambar along with sika deer, have been raised in farms for their antlers, which are highly prised for use as knife handles and as grips for handguns.

Reproduction

Males establish a territory from which they attract nearby females, but males do not establish a harem. The male stomps the ground, creating a bare patch, and often wallows in the mud, perhaps to accentuate the colour of his hair, which is typically darker than that of females. They have been heard to make a loud sound. Large, dominant stags defend nonexclusive territories surrounded by several smaller males, with which they have bonded and formed alliances. Sambars lock antlers, when sparring with rival males and push. They also sometimes stand on their hind legs and clash downward into each other. Females also fight on their hind legs and use their fore legs to hit each other in the head. Courtship is based more on tending bonds rather than males vocally advertising themselves. Mating and reproduction occurs year round. When mounting, males do not clasp. The front legs of the male hang loosely and intromission takes the form of a 'copulatory jump'. Oestrus lasts around 18 days. Gestation lasts around 8 months. Normally, only one calf is born at a time. The calve weighs 5 to 8 kg. Sambars have lived up to 28 years in captivity, although they survive about 12 years in the wild.

Threats and Conservation

Sambar is listed as Vulnerable on the IUCN Red List since 2008. Populations have declined considerably due to severe hunting, and habitat loss due to industrial exploitation of their habitat. They are favourite prey of tigers, Asiatic lions, Dhole and Dogs and crocodiles. Sambar forms main diet of Bengal tiger (Panthera tigris). Males try to defend from predators with their antlers.

Despite their lack of antlers, female sambar try to defend their young from most predators, especially from Dogs and pack-hunting dholes by lowering their heads with an erect mane and lashes. Sambar prefers to defend the attack from predators in shallow water. Several Sambars may form a defensive formation, touching rumps and vocalising loudly at the dogs. When sensing danger, a sambar stamps its feet and makes a ringing call known as "pooking" or "belling".

Protected areas, such as wildlife sanctuary, National Parks and Biosphere Reserves are used to conserve Sambars.

Chapter - 19

The State Animal of Rajasthan: Chinkara (*Gazelia bennettii*)

Gazelia bennettii, IUCN: VU (Vulnerable), Indian Wildlife Act: Schedule I, Cites:I

Kingdom	:	Animalia
Phylum	:	Chordata
Class	:	Mammalia
Order	:	Artiodactyla
Family	:	Bovidae
Subfamily	:	Antilopinae
Genus	:	*Gazella*
Species	:	*Gazella bennettii*

Chinkara is called Indian Gazella is a small slender built beautiful Antelope. They are native to Iran, Pakistan and India. Six subspecies have been identified.

Body Weight

Its height is about 65 cm at shoulder and it weighs about 25 kg. The body colour is light chestnut or light brown. The ventral part of the body is white in colour. It has a short black hair tail, always wagging. The horn is slightly curved. The horn contains ring like structure from the origin up to the tip. The horns in males are larger than the horns in females. They live in groups of 04-20 animals. Chinkara can run very fast.

Ecology

Chinkara is found in low hill habitats or plains of Rajasthan, Haryana and *north-western part and central part of India.* Chinkara live in arid plains and hills, deserts (Desert National Park, Rajasthan), dry scrub and thin forests. They inhabit more than 80 protected areas in India. In 2001, the Indian Chinkara population was estimated at eighty thousand to one lakh individuals living in the Thar Desert of Rajasthan. Chinkara are shy and avoid human habitation.

They get sufficient fluids from plants and dew and therefore, they can go without water for long periods. They are seen sometimes in groups of four animals. They share their habitat with several other herbivores, such as Nilgai, Blackbuck, Chawsingha, Wild goats, and Wild pigs.

Its food is mainly grass and crops, fruits such as melon and pumpkin. They can withstand long period without drinking water as they get water from plants and fruits and dew.

Reproduction

Chinkara mate once a year. Males compete for possession for females.

Threats and Conservation

Chinkara are preyed upon by their natural predators such as

leopards, Bengal tigers, dholes, wolves and golden jackals. Outside protected areas they may be attacked by pariah dogs.

The Chinkara is threatened by extensive hunting for meat and their skull used as decorative materials. Other threats include habitat loss due to agricultural and industrial expansion. However, the situation in India is not so grim. In 2001, populations were estimated at over one million in the country, of which nearly 80,000 to one lakh occurred in the Thar Desert.

The Chinkara occurs in over 80 protected areas in India. In January 2016, the Karnataka government issued a notification to establish a sanctuary especially for Chinkara in the Yadahalli village in the Bagalkot district of the state. This region shelters a major population of Chinkara.

Chinkara is protected in nine areas of Iran and five of Pakistan.

Since 2003, it has been listed as Vulnerable on the IUCN Red List.

Chapter -20

The State Animal of Sikkim: *Red Panda* (Ailurus fulgens*)*

Red Panda (Ailurus fulgens (F. Cuvier)
IUCN : EN (Endangered), India: Schedule I. Cites: I

Kingdom	:	Animalia
Phylum	:	Chordata
Class	:	Mammalia
Order	:	Carnivora
Family	:	Ailuridae
Genus	:	*Ailurus* F. Cuvier, 1825
Species	:	Ailurus fulgens

Red Panda is also called Lesser Panda. They belong to the family Procyonidae having one species namely *Ailurus fulgens,* called *red panda.*Two subspecies have been recognised. They are (i) Western red panda *A. fulgens fulgens* (Cuvier, 1825) lives in the western part of its range, in Nepal, Bhutan, and Indian north-eastern states particularly in Assam, Meghalaya, Sikkim, (ii) Styan's red panda *A. f. styani* lives in southern China and northern Myanmar.

Body Structure

The body length of a red panda measures 50 to 64 cm, and its tail is 28 to 59 cm. Males weigh 3.7 to 6.2 kg and females 3 to 6.0 kg. They have long, soft, reddish brown fur on the upper parts of the body, and blackish fur on the lower parts. Their soft fur serves as thermal insulation on snow-covered surfaces and conceals scent glands, which are also present on the anus.They have a light face with tear markings (white badges) with robust cranio dental features. The sides of the eye and mouth are white in colour. Each individual may have distinctive markings. Their heads are roundish with medium-sized upright ears and black noses and pointed snout. Eyes are black. They have long, bushy tails with six alternating transverse ochre rings. Tail is brown with black and pale rings. The body and tail colour provide excellent camouflage against their habitat of mossand lichen-covered trees and the tail provides balance. The legs are black and short with thick fur on the soles of the paws. They have short legs with feet containing sharp and retractable claws. They have features like a cat and a bear; hence called cat-bear.

Ecology

The red panda is endemic to the temperate forests of the Himalayas. Its range of occurrence is from southern Tibet, Sikkim and north-east in India, Bhutan, the northern mountains of Myanmar, and in south-western China. A population inhabits the Meghalaya Plateau of north-eastern India.

They are found in pairs or single. It is mainly solitary except during mating season. They can climb trees very fast as they have claws and they rest in a branch of a tree with belly lying on the top of the branch and legs dangling in mid air. They are arboreal, nocturnal and active from dusk to dawn. While descending a tree, the red panda rotates its ankle to control its descent, one of the few climbing species to do so. The species is generally quiet except for some twittering, tweeting, and whistling communication sounds. It has been reported to be both nocturnal and crepuscular, sleeping on tree branches or in tree hollows during the day and increasing its activity in the late afternoon and early evening hours. They mark their territories, marking with urine and a weak musk-smelling secretion from their anal glands.

Food

The red panda lives between 2,200 and 4,800 m altitude, in areas of moderate temperature between 10 and 25°C. It prefers mountainous forests with mixed deciduous and conifer trees especially with old trees and dense under stories of bamboo. They feed on bamboo shoots, root tubers, succulent plants, and fruits and on bird eggs, insects and small vertebrates. The red panda is specialised as a bamboo feeder with strong, curved and sharp semi-retractile claws standing inward for grasping narrow tree branches, leaves, and fruit.

Red pandas digest bamboo poorly, especially the cellulose and cell wall components as they do not have cellulase enzyme in the gut and the density of microorganisms secreting cellulase is not adequate. Bamboo shoots are more easily digested than leaves, exhibiting the highest digestibility in summer and autumn, intermediate digestibility in the spring, and lowest digestibility in the winter. These variations correlate with the nutrient contents in the bamboo. This also implies microbial digestion plays a minor role in their digestive strategy. To survive on this poor-quality diet, they have to eat the high-quality sections of the bamboo plant, such as the tender leaves containing less percentage of cellulose. Each adult consumes over 1.5 kg of fresh leaves and 4 kg of fresh shoots daily. This food passes through the digestive tract fairly rapidly so as to maximise daily nutrient intake. Red pandas can taste artificial sweeteners, such as aspartame, and are the only non-primates known to be able to do so (based on wikipedia).They may eat small mammals, flowers, and berries. They were observed in captivity, to eat flowers, maple and mulberry leaves, and bark and fruits of maple, beech, and mulberry and birds. They also eat mushrooms, roots, acorns, lichens, and grasses to supplement their nutrient requirement. It exhibits peculiar behaviour like cats in cleaning its sole of the foot, and with sole, they clean the fur. Drinking habit is peculiar as it plunges its paw into water and then licks the paw. Sometimes they use their snout to suck the water into mouth. They produce peculiar sound like cats, sometimes like bears and sometimes like dogs while eating. People kill them to collect its fur and to sale to the Zoos.

Reproduction

Red pandas reproduce at around 18 months of age, and the young ones become mature at two to three years. The mating season is from mid-January to mid-March. Both sexes may mate with more than one partner during the mating season. A few days before birth, females begin to collect material, such as brushwood, grass, and leaves, to build a nest, which is normally located in a hollow of a tree or a rock crevice. After a gestation period of 112 to 158 days, the female gives birth in mid-June to late July to one to four (usually 1-2) blind and deaf cubs weighing 110 to 130 g each.

After birth, the mother cleans the cubs. Mother recognises each young one by its smell. In the first week after birth, she spends up to 90 per cent of her time with the cubs to nurse them. After the first week, the mother starts spending more time outside the nest to eat and collect food for her, returning every few hours to nurse the cubs. She moves the young frequently among several nests, all of which she keeps clean. The young ones start to open their eyes at about 18 days of age. By about 90 days, they have achieved full adult fur and colouring, and begin to venture out of the nest. They also start eating solid foods at this point, weaning at around six to eight months of age. The cubs stay with their mother until the next litter is born in the following summer. Males rarely help raise the young. Males help only if they live in pairs or in small groups. The red panda has a low birth rate and a high death rate in the wild.

A red panda's average lifespan is between eight and 10 years, but individuals have been known to reach 15 years.

Threats and Conservation

Predators of the red panda include the snow leopard, and humans.

When facing danger from predators, they may try to escape by climbing a tree or rock column. If they can no longer flee, they stand on their hind legs to make themselves appear larger and use their sharp claws on the front paws to defend themselves.

Its wild population is estimated in India was estimated in 2001 at between 5,000 and 6,000 individuals and worldwide at less than 20,000 mature individuals and continues to decline due to habitat loss and fragmentation, poaching, and inbreeding depression. The relative importance of these factors is different in each region. In the past, red pandas were captured and sold to zoos. In some parts of Nepal and India, red pandas are kept as pets.

India has 20 protected areas with known or estimated red panda populations in Sikkim, Arunachal Pradesh, and West Bengal such as Khangchendzonga National Park, Namdapha National Park, and Singalila National Park, and a coordinated conservation policy for the red panda.Villagers in the high altitude areas of Arunachal Pradesh have formed the Pangchen Red Panda Conservation Alliance comprising five villages with a community-conserved forest area of 200 km^2 at an altitude of 2,500 m to over 4,000 m. This has tourism potential.

Red pandas are protected by national laws in India. The red panda has been classified as Endangered by the IUCN and is listed in CITES Appendix I.

Chapter - 21

The State Animal of Tamil Nadu: Nilgiri Tahr (Nilgiritragus (=Hemitragus) *hylocrius*)

Nilgiri Tahr (Nilgiritragus (=Hemitragus)* hylocrius*),
IUCN: EN (Endangered), India: Schedule I.

Kingdom	:	Animalia
Phylum	:	Chordata
Class	:	Mammalia
Order	:	Artiodactyla
Family	:	Bovidae
Genus	:	Nilgiritragus
Species	:	Nilgiritragus hylocrius

Two species of Tahr or mountain goats are found in India. They are the Himalayan Tahr (*Hemitragus jemlahicus*) and the Nilgiri Tahr (*Nilgiritragus hylocrius*). In Himalayas, they live in altitudes ranging from 2500 m to 4400 m and Nilgiri mountain range including Tamil Nadu, they are found in altitudes 1300 m to 2600 m. The Nilgiri Tahr is larger in size than the Himalayan Tahr. The Nilgiri tahr, known locally as the Nilgiri ibex. Despite its local name, it is more closely related to the sheep of the *Ovis* genus and wild goats of the *Capra* genus than the Ibex. This species is endemic to the Nilgiri Hills and the southern portion of the Western Ghats in the states of Tamil Nadu and Kerala. It is the state animal of Tamil Nadu. It is a stocky goat with short, coarse fur and a bristly mane.

Body Structure

Their body colour is grey or brownish-grey (young animals) and in aged animals the colour is black. Females and young one may look yellowish-grey. It is a strong and fast moving goat of mountains. Both sexes have curved horns, and the two horns are curved towards back and contain ring like structures in the horns. The horns are about 40 cm long in males and about 30 cm long in females. Adult males weigh about 80 to 100 kg. Females are smaller than males. Adult male stands about 100 cm tall at the shoulder.

Ecology

The Nilgiri tahr inhabits the open montane grassland habitat and in the mountain forests open into grasslands interspersed with pockets of stunted forests, locally called as *sholas*. They live in groups of five to fifty animals and graze on grasses and other plants.

Threats and Conservation

Their population has been reduced considerably because of excessive poaching and they have become threatened. Only one hundred or so Nilgiri Tahr was found in the first half of twentieth century. Recent population estimate by WWF, India is about 3122 individuals. Wildlife census conducted by Kerala forest department in association with College of Forestry & Veterinary Science under Kerala Agricultural University, in 2014, mention the number of animals as 894 individuals in Eravikulam National Park. The other sizable concentration of Nilgiri Tahr is in the Nilgiri Hills, Anamalai Hills, Periyar National Park,

Palni Hills and in some pockets of Western Ghats. Smaller size population inhabit Kanyakumari district of Tamil Nadu and Ponmudi hills of Tiruvantapuram district of Kerala. The species is classified by IUCN: EN (Endangered), India: Schedule I.

Chapter - 22

The State Animal of Telengana: Spotted Deer (Axis axis)

Spotted Deer (**Axis axis*****) IUCN: LC (Least Concerned), India: Schedule III***

Kingdom	:	Animalia
Phylum	:	Chordata
Class	:	Mammalia
Order	:	Artiodactyla
Family	:	Cervidae
Genus	:	Axis (C.H.Smith,1827)
Species	:	Axis axis

The chital or cheetal (*Axis axis*), also known as spotted deer is native of the Indian subcontinent. In 1777, the spotted Deer was first described by German naturalist Erxleben. The scientific name of the chital is *Axis axis*. "Axis" has the origin in Sanskrit '*akṣah*'. The vernacular name chital is derived from the Sanskrit *citrala*, meaning spotted or bright, in Hindi *cītal*. It refers to the spotted coat of the deer. The species is considered monotypic. The beautiful spotted Deer is found in most of the states except in the plains of Rajasthan and Punjab.

Body Structure

A moderate-sized deer, male chital reach nearly 90 centimetres and females 70 centimetres at the shoulder. The head-and-body length is around 1.7 metres. The males weigh 30–75 kg and the females weigh 25–45 kg. They are sexually dimorphic. Males are larger and possess about one metre long and three-pronged antlers and females are comparatively of smaller size and without antlers. Each of the antlers has three lines on it. The brow tine (the first division in the antler) is roughly perpendicular to the beam (the central stalk of the antler). The antlers emerge as soft tissues (known as velvet antlers) and progressively harden due to mineralisation into bony structures (known as hard antlers). Blood vessels are blocked in the tissue, from the tip to the base. A study of the mineral composition of the antlers of captive chital, barasinga, and hog deer showed that the horns of the deer are similar with respect to the mineral content such as 6.1 mg/kg copper, 8.04 mg/kg cobalt, and 32.14 mg/kg zinc.

The Chital have well-developed preorbital glands (near the eyes) and welldeveloped metatarsal glands and pedal glands located in their hind legs. The preorbital glands are larger in males than in females, and the glands frequently open in response to certain stimuli.

The upper parts of the Deer are golden colour, and completely covered with white spots. The abdomen, throat, insides of legs, ears and tail are all white in colour.

Ecology

Chital are found throughout India but they have become extinct in north-east of India. Chital are active throughout the day and activity peaks as dusk approaches. Foraging begins before sunrise and peaks by early morning and again in the late afternoon till midnight. In the summer, day time is spent in rest under shade of trees. In search of foraging sites and water sources, they move in a single file on specific tracks. They fall asleep a few hours before sunrise. The chital is found in large numbers in dense deciduous or semi-evergreen forests and open grasslands.

The chital forms matriarchal herds, usually small herds comprising an adult female and her offspring of the previous and the present year, with individuals of any age and either sex, male herds and herds of juveniles and mothers. However, herds of size 50-100 individuals have been observed. Rutting males leave their herds during the mating season, hence herd composition changes. Large herds were most common in monsoon, observed foraging in the grasslands.

A study in the Gir National Park (Gujarat, India) showed that cheetal travel the most in summer of all seasons for search of forage area. Facing the potential danger if any. Chital cautiously inspecting its vicinity, will stand motionless and hear the sound with rapt attention. This stance is usually adopted by nearby individuals as well. As an anti-predator measure, chital will flee in groups and sprints are often followed by hiding in dense undergrowth. While running chital has its tail raised, exposing the white underparts. They usually stay/graze within 300 metres of cover. There is vocalisation in deer in form of coarse bellows and loud growls as alarm barks.

Food

Chital graze when grasses are available, else they browse tree leaves. The cheetal mainly feed on grasses and browse on tree leaves throughout the year. They browse edible vegetation from the hanging branches of trees and graze on grass. Browsing includes herbs, shrubs, foliage, and fruits. Browsing forms a major part of the diet in winter months (October to January), when grasses dry up, and become non-palatable. Cheetal prefer young shoots. Coarse grasses are nibbled off at the tips. Fruits of Ficus sp., Syzygium *cumini* , and *Cordia myxa* eaten by chital. Water sources are visited nearly twice daily, with great caution. Salt licks rich in calcium and phosphorus pentoxide are scrapped by the incisor teeth. In Sunderbans, West Bengal, remains of red crabs have been found in the rumen of Cheetal.

Females and juveniles will bark persistently when alarmed or if they encounter a predator. The chital responds to the alarm calls of common myna and langurs and some other animals.

Male Cheetal browsing on tree leaves

Reproduction

Marking behaviour is pronounced in males. Males have well-developed preorbital glands. They stand on their hindlegs to reach tall branches for foraging and rub the open preorbital glands to deposit their scent there. Urine-marking is also observed; the smell of urine is typically stronger than that of the deposited scent.

Larger male displaying dominance before the other by hissing, heading away from the other male with the tail facing him, the nose pointing to the ground, the ears down, the antlers upright and the upper lip raised. The fur often bristles during the display. The male approaches the other in a slow gait. The opponents then interlock their horns and push against each other. The fight terminates with the males stepping backward, or simply leaving and then foraging. Fights are not generally serious. Breeding takes place throughout the year. Males with hard antlers are dominant over those without antlers irrespective of their size. A rutting male fasts during the mating season and follow and guard a female in oestrus. Dominant males guarding females in oestrus making high-pitched growls at less powerful males. Males may moan during aggressive displays or while resting Females have regular oestrus cycles, each lasting three weeks. The pair will do several bouts of chasing and mutual licking before copulation. Courtship is based on tending bonds. Males produce sperms year-round, except less production during the development of the antlers.

Copulating cheetal

Mother with her fawn

The female can conceive again two weeks to four months after the birth of a fawn(s). The newborn is hidden for a week after birth. The mother-fawn bond is not very strong. The average lifespan in captivity is nearly 22 years. The longevity in the wild, is about ten years.

Threat and Conservation

It also runs fast, especially when chased by predator like tiger or leopard. Hooves measure between 4.1 and 6.1 centimetres in length; hooves of the forelegs are longer than those of the hindlegs. The toes taper to a point. This helps them to run fast. The chital can leap and clear fences as high as 1.5 metres, but prefers to dive under them.

Along with Sambar, this deer forms the main food of tigers and leopards in jungles.

Altruistic Behaviour

Common myna and gray langurs are often attracted to the chital. An interesting relationship has been observed between herds of chital and troops of the northern plains gray langurs, (Presbytes entellus). Chital benefit from the langurs' eyesight and ability to post a lookout from trees, while the langur benefit from the chital's strong sense of smell-both of which help keep a check on potential danger, especially tigers and leopards. The chital also benefit from fruits dropped by langurs from trees such as *Terminalia bellerica* and *Phyllanthus emblica*.

Chapter - 23

The State Animal of Tripura: Phayre's langur (*Trachypithecus phayrei*)

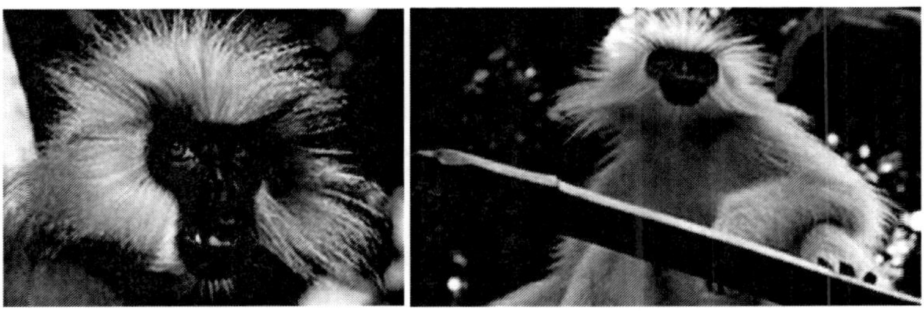

Phayre's langur (*Trachypithecus phayrei*), *Trachypithecus gee-*Golden langur, IUCN: EN (Endangered), India: Schedule I

Kingdom	:	Animalia
Phylum	:	Chordata
Class	:	Mammalia
Order	:	Primates
Family	:	Cercopithecidae
Genus	:	*Trachypithecus*
Species	:	T. phayrei (Blyth,1847)

The Phayre's leaf monkey (*Trachypithecus phayrei*), also known as Phayre's langur, is found in Southeast Asia including Tripura, Assam and in the neighbouring of Black mountain of Bhutan. Its range includes Bangladesh, India, Myanmar, China, Thailand, Laos and Vietnam. This species has three subspecies namely: *Trachypithecus phayrei, T. crepusculus and T. shanicus.* Phayre's langur is also called golden langur along with *Trachypithecus gee.*

The scientific discovery of golden langur monkeys in central region of Bhutan was made by Griffith as mentioned by Pemberton in his paper published in 1838. It was rediscovered in 1970 by scientists. Later, a pale yellow coloured langur, common in the adjoining district of Goalpara (Assam) was discovered. E. P. Gee and his team observed three groups of golden langur in 1953 in Bhutan and adjacent areas of India. Scientists of Zoological Survey of India, when Dr. Sunder Lal Hora was the Director, collected six specimens of golden langur from Assam and neighbouring region in 1954. The following year, Dr. H. Khajuria, a taxonomist in ZSI, who studied the specimens, described the new species naming it *Presbystis geei* in honour of Gee. At present after detailed study, it is recognised that the golden langur has three subspecies as described above and *Trachypithecus phayrei has been named as the state animal of Tripura.* The regions of its distribution of golden monkey are very small; limited to an area approximately 100 km sq bounded on the south by the Brahmaputra River, on the east by the Manas River, on the west by the Sankosh River, all in Assam, and on the north by the Black Mountains of Bhutan, and lesser abundance region in a small portion of the northwestern part of Tripura state. These biogeographical barriers are believed to have led to the radiation of species from the closely related capped langur (*Trachypithecus pileatus*).

Body Structure

The coat colour of the adult golden langur varies from cream to golden; on its flanks. The chest hairs are darker and often rust white colour. The coats of the females and juveniles are lighter, silvery white to light buff. The golden langur has a black face and a long tail measuring up to 50 cm in length.

Ecology

It is mostly arboreal, and its long tail serves as a balancer when it leaps across branches. Golden langur lives in troops of about four to

22 individuals with several females to each adult male. The smallest golden langur troop was composed of four individuals, while the largest had 22. The sex ratio is more than two females to every male. However, most of the majority troops had only one dominant adult male.

Diet

They feed on leaves of a large number of tree species. In Tripura, it is found that the principal food tree species to be *Albizzia procera*, *Melocanna bambusoides*, *Callicarpa arborea*, *Dillenia pentagyna*, *Litsea* sp., *Albizzia lebbek*, *Mikania scandens*, *Gmelina arborea*, *Artocarpus chaplasha*, *Syzygium fruticosum*, *Ficus fistulosa*, *Ficus racemosa*, *Ficus hispida*, *Ficus indica*, *Macaranga denticulata* and *Albizzia stipulata.* It obtains its water requirement from dew and rain drenched leaves. Its diet is herbivorous, consisting of young and mature leaves, seeds, buds and flowers, and fruits.

Threat and Conservation

The golden langur is IUCN endangered species and Indian Schedule I species. In 1988, two captive groups of golden langurs were released into two protected areas of Tripura state. As of 2000, one of these groups, consisting of six to eight individuals in the Sepahijala Wildlife Sanctuary, has survived.

A total Indian population recorded in 2001 was 1,064 individuals, in 130 groups. Of these, approximately 60 per cent were adults and it indicated less number of juveniles and infants, which in turn indicated a declining population. The reason of declining population was human activities and may be predation by leopards. A fragmented but protected population of golden langur in a rubber plantation in Nayakgaon, Kokrajhar district of Assam increased in population from 38 individuals in 1997 to 52 in 2002. The population has also adapted to feeding on dry rubber seeds.

In view of these findings, Golden langur requires protection for survival.

Chapter - 24

The State Animal of Uttarakhand: Alpine Musk deer (Moschus *chrysogaster*)

Alpine Musk Deer (Moschus* chrysogaster*)
IUCN Category: LR/nt, Cites I

India	:	Schedule I
Kingdom	:	Animalia
Phylum	:	Chordata
Class	:	Mammalia
Order	:	Artiodactyla

Family	:	Moschidae
Genus	:	*Moschus*
Species	:	*Moschus chrysogaste*

The male Deer has a musk gland near the tail. The gland lies in a sac located between the genitals and the umbilicus. Its secretions are most likely used to attract females for mating. Musk has commercial value as it is used in perfumes and considered as an aphrodisiac and hence the deer is poached by people. It is an endangered species and needs protection for survival.

Body Structure

The Musk Deer does not have horns. It is a small deer with a stocky build, and hind legs longer than their front legs. It is dark brown in colour and the coat has bristly hair. It measures about 50 to 70 cm at the shoulder and about 80-100 cm long. The body weight varies between 7 and 17 kg. The feet of musk deer are adapted for climbing in rough terrain in mountains. The musk deer family differs from true deer, by lacking antlers and facial glands and by possessing only a single pair of teats and a pair of tusk-like teeth resembling canine teeth, forming sabre like tusks. The dental formula in musk deer is similar to that of other deer species i.e. 0 1 3 3 / 3 1 3 3 (order is incisor, canine, premolar and molar in upper and lower jaw respectively).

Ecology

Musk deer live mainly in forested and alpine scrub habitats in the Himalayas. They are entirely Asian in their present distribution, being extinct in Europe where the earliest musk deer are known to have existed from Oligocene deposits. Alpine Musk deer is found on barren plateaus at high altitudes, where it occupies meadows, scrub lands or fir forests. They prefer shaded steeper slopes with less human disturbance. They inhabit in altitudes ranging from 2000 m to 4,500 m.

Population density estimations are not done by rigorous scientific methods. Some reports based on pellet counts suggested that their population in the world was about 1,80,000 individuals between 1960 and 1970 and some other reports indicate less than one lakh individuals in China in 1990s. Recent estimates of their population in

Sagarmatha National Park in Nepal indicate 600-800 individuals with a density of 45- 71 individuals/km^2 and few hundred animals in other national parks in Nepal. The alpine musk is also found in Annapurna and Kanchenjunga Conservation Areas, Dhorpatan Hunting Reserve Khaptad National Park and Makulu-Barun National Park. Outside of protected areas the species is declining.

Diet

They are herbivores and they brows or graze on leaves, grasses, flowers, mosses and lichens. They are solitary animals and are shy and mostly nocturnal. Musk deer is predominantly a browser, feeding mainly on shrubs, forbs, leaves, moss, lichens, shoots, grasses and twigs. The proportion of leaves and tender shoots in the diet is highest in spring and summer, buds and flowers in late summer, and leaves, twigs and flowers of forbs and shrubs later in the year.

Reproduction

Males maintain territories. For breeding purpose they compete with other males using their tusks for getting mates. The territories are scent marked with their caudal glands. Breeding occurs in November-December. Offspring are born during May to June. The newborn fawn are very small, and essentially motionless for the first month of their lives, a feature that helps them remain hidden from predators. After birth, fawns lie hidden in secluded areas, mothers visiting at feeding times. The hiding period may last up to two months. Gestation period is from 150-195 days and females give birth usually to one offspring. Fawns wean at 3-4 months, and become sexually mature at 16-24 months.

Threat and Conservation

The main natural predators are the fox, wolf, snow leopard, and other predators. Musk deer emit a loud double hiss if alarmed. The musk produced by this Deer is highly valued for its cosmetic and pharmaceutical properties, and its price is US $45,000 per kg on the international market. Musk can be extracted from live male animals; but most "musk-gatherers" kill the animals to remove the entire sac, which yields only about 25 grams of the brown waxy substance. Such poaching is relatively easy to accomplish and difficult to stop using only legal means and it is the principal threat in Uttarakhand.

Musk deer also requires dense vegetation, but excessive forest clearance or grazing by domestic cattle is another threat.

This species is listed on CITES Appendix I in India, IUCN: En (Endangered), India: Schedule I.

Chapter - 25

The State Animal of West Bengal: Fishing Cat (*Prionailurus* viverrinus)

Fishing Cat: (Prionailurus viverrinus), IUCN Category: VU (Vulnerable), India: Schedule I

Scientific Classification

Kingdom	:	Animalia
Phylum	:	Chordata
Class	:	Mammalia
Order	:	Carnivora
Family	:	Felidae
Genus	:	*Prionailurus*
Species	:	P. viverrinus (Bennett, 1833)

The fishing cat is the state animal of West Bengal.
Since 2016, it is listed as Vulnerable on the IUCN Red List.

The Fishing Cat (Prionailurus viverrinus) is a medium-sized wild cat of South and Southeast Asia but largest of the *Prionailurus* cats. It is about twice the size of a domestic cat.

Body Structure

Its coarse fur is olive-grey to ashy-grey in colour with darker stripes on the shoulder and roundish or oval-shaped spots on the flanks and sides. The ears are short and round and lie low on the head. The back of the ears have a white spot. Two stripes are on the cheeks, and four stripes run from above the eyes between the ears to the shoulder.

The underside is white, and two rows of spots are found around the throat. The underside fur is longer and often overlaid with spots. It has a short tail, less than half the length of head and body. The tail is spotted at the base and with a few black rings at the end. The tail is of 20 to 30 cm long.

It is stocky and muscular. Its face is elongated. Its head-to-body length typically ranges from 57 to 78 cm. Its body weighs varies from 5 to 16 kg. Its paws are webbed and the claws are incompletely sheathed so that they protrude slightly when retracted. Webbed feet have often been noted as a characteristic of the fishing cat, but the webbing beneath the toes is not much more developed.

Ecology

Fishing cat populations are threatened by destruction of wetlands and declined severely over the last decade. Fishing cats live foremost in the vicinity of wetlands, along rivers, streams, in swamps and mangroves such as Sunderban in West Bengal.

In India, the presence of fishing cats has been documented in Ranthambhore Tiger Reserve, in Sur Sarovar Bird Sanctuary, outside protected areas in West Bengal, in and around Krishna Wildlife Sanctuary, in Coringa Wildlife Sanctuary and adjoining reserve forests in Andhra Pradesh, and Bhittarkanika mangroves of Odisha. The fishing cat is discontinuously distributed in Asia, and also found in the Terai region of the Himalayan foothills in India and Nepal, Bangladesh and Sri Lanka, Thailand, Cambodia, Sindh Province of Pakistan.

Fishing cats are primarily nocturnal. Adult males and females are solitary animals. They spend considerable time in the water bodies and they are good swimmers and can swim long distances. They can swim even under water. The females range over an areas of 4 to 6 km^2, while males range over 16 to 22 km^2). Adults have been observed to make a "chuckling" sound.

Diet

Their main prey is fish; but they can eat birds, rodents, mollusks, insects, frogs and toads and nonpoisonous snakes.

Reproductive

Males mark their territory by urine-spraying and by rubbing cheek, head, chin, neck and to leave scent marks. The mating season is during January and February; and the kittens in the wild were observed during March and April. In captivity, the gestation period lasts 63–70 days. Females give birth to two or three kittens. The kittens weigh around 170 gram at birth, and are able to actively move around by the age of one month. They begin to play in water and to take solid food when about two months of age. They are not fully weaned until six months old. They reach full adult size in eight to nine months. Canine teeth develop fully by 11 months. They become sexually mature when approximately 15 months old. Their longevity is on the average ten years in captivity.

Threats and Conservation

Fishing cats are threatened by destruction of wetlands, which are increasingly being polluted and converted for agricultural use and human settlements. In many places target killing is prevalent because of human/fishing cat conflict for getting fish and their skin. The fishing cat will be extinct unless conservation measures are taken. Hunting is prohibited in India, Bangladesh, Cambodia, China, Indonesia, Myanmar, Nepal, Pakistan, and Sri Lanka, Captive breeding programmes as a measure of conservation have been established by the European Association of Zoos and Aquaria and the American Association of Zoos and Aquariums. All the fishing cats kept in zoos around the world are listed in the International Studybook of the World Association of Zoos and Aquariums.

Chapter - 26

Andaman & Nicobar Islands: Sea Cow (Dugong), *Dugong dugong* Lacépède, 1799

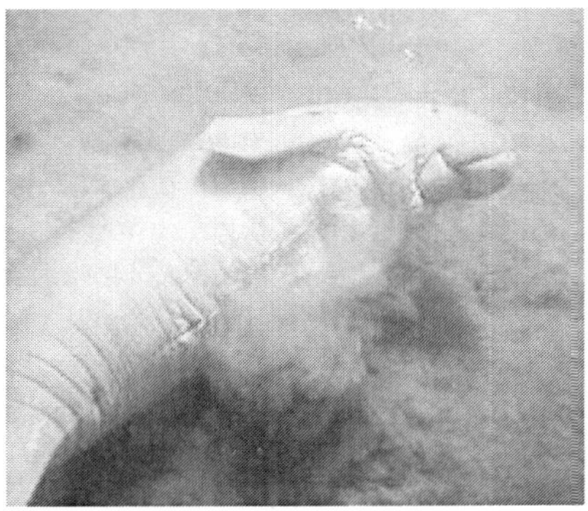

Sea Cow (Dugong) Dugong on the sea floor

IUCN: VU (Vulnerable), India: Schedule I.

Dugongs

Kingdom	:	Animalia
Phylum	:	Chordata
Class	:	Mammalia
Order	:	Sirenia
Family	:	Dugongidae

Genus	:	Dugong Lacépède, 1799
Species	:	*Dugong dugong*

The dugong is a medium to large-sized marine mammal. It is close to modern relative, Steller's sea cow (*Hydrodamalis gigas*), which was hunted to extinction in the eighteenth century. The word "dugong" was adopted from the Malay *duyung*, meaning "lady of the sea". Other common local popular names include "sea cow", "sea pig" and "sea camel". Dugongs and elephants share a monophyletic group. The dugong is the only marine herbivorous mammal.

Body Structure

The dugong has a fusiform body with no dorsal fin or hind limbs. The dugong's body is large with a cylindrical shape that tapers at both ends. It has thick, smooth skin that is a pale cream colour at birth, but darkens dorsally and laterally to brownish-to-dark-grey with age. The colour of a dugong can change due to the growth of marine algae on the skin. The body is sparsely covered in short hair and these hairs are most developed around the mouth, which has a large horseshoe-shaped upper lip forming a highly mobile muzzle. This muscular upper lip aids the dugong in foraging. The flippers or forelimbs of *dugong* are paddle-like. The dugong has fluked, dolphin-like tail, but also possesses a unique skull and teeth. Its snout is sharply downturned, an adaptation for feeding in benthic seagrass communities. The molar teeth are simple and peg-like.

The skull is enlarged with sharply down-turned. The spine has between 57 and 60 vertebrae.The dugong has two incisors teeth (tusks) which emerge in males during puberty. The female's tusks continue to grow and may not emerge fully during puberty. It may emerge later in life. The number of growth layer in a tusk indicates the age of a dugong. The cheek-teeth move forward with age. The dental formula of dugongs is 2, 0, 3, 3: 3,1,3,3. It means that they have two incisors, three premolars, and three molars teeth on each side of their upper jaw, and three incisors, one canine, three premolars, and three molars on each side of their lower jaw, a total of 36 teeth.

The dugong experiences pachyostosis, a condition in which the ribs and other long bones are unusually solid and contain little or no bone-marrow. These heavy bones, which are among the densest in the animal kingdom, act as a ballast helping to remain suspended slightly below the water's surface.

An adult's body length is about 3 metres. The body weight in adults varies between 250 kg to about 900 kg. The largest individual so far recorded was 4.06 metres long and weighed 1,016 kg, and was found off the Saurashtra coast of western part of India. Females tend to be larger than males.

The dugong's tail flukes and flippers are raised up and down in long strokes to move the animal forward, and can be twisted to turn. The forelimbs are paddle-like flippers which aid in turning and slowing. The dugong lacks nails on its flippers, which are only 15 per cent of a dugong's body length. The tail has deep notches. A dugong's brain is small, weighs only maximum of 300 g, about 0.1 per cent of the animal's body weight. With very small eyes, dugongs have limited vision. Their ears are located on the sides of their head and lack pinnae. They have acute hearing ability within narrow sound thresholds. The nostrils are located on top of the head and they have valves to close and open the nostrils. The lungs in a dugong are very long, extending almost as far

Dugong tail fluke

as the kidneys, which are also highly elongated in order to cope with the saltwater environment. They can go six minutes without breathing (about two and a half minutes is more typical), and have been known to rest on their tail to breathe with their heads above water. Blood clots rapidly if a dugong is wounded.

Ecology

It is found in marine waters of some 37 countries throughout the Indo-Pacific region and in Andaman and Nicobar Island waters. Dugongs are generally found in warm waters around the coast with large numbers concentrated in wide and shallow protected bays. Dugongs are widely distributed in warm coastal waters from the western Pacific Ocean to the eastern coast of Africa, between 26° and 27° degrees to the north and south of the equator. Their range of distribution corresponds to the occurrence of that of sea grasses from the Potamogetonaceae and Hydrocharitaceae families. At present populations of dugongs are found in the waters of 37 countries and territories. However, the dugong population is thought to be declining. At present the northern waters of Australia between Shark Bay and Moreton Bay are believed to be the dugong's stronghold. They can tolerate the brackish waters found in coastal wetlands, and large numbers are also found in wide and shallow mangrove channels of large inshore islands, where seagrass beds are common. They are usually located at a depth of around 10 m although in areas where the continental shelf remains shallow dugongs have been known to travel more than 10 km from the shore, descending to as far as 37 m, if deepwater seagrasses such as *Halophila spinulosa* are found. They are usually solitary or found in pairs. Gatherings of large number of dugongs sometimes happen, but they disperse after short time. They can dive to a maximum depth of 39 metres. They spend most of their lives no deeper than 10 metres.

The Marine National Park, Gulf of Kutch houses the only remaining population in western India. A depleted population exists in the Gulf of Mannar Marine National Park and the Palk Strait between India and Sri Lanka, but the population density is not known. Good growth of seagrass beds is available in the Chilika Lake in Odisha, raising hopes for re-colorisations of dugong. The population around the

Andaman and Nicobar Islands are known only from a few records. It is now believed to be small and scattered.

Diet

Dugong is the only marine herbivorous mammal. The dugong is largely dependent on seagrass communities for its food. Therefore, it is restricted to the coastal habitats which support seagrass meadows. The largest dugong concentrations occur in shallow, protected areas such as bays, mangrove channels, the waters of large inshore islands and inter-reefal waters in different places including Andaman and Nicobar Islands. If the sea grasses are in short supply, they eat invertebrates such as jellyfish, sea squirts, shellfish and Polychaetes.This situation does not normally prevail in tropical waters and hence they depend mainly on sea grasses.

Reproductive Biology

A male's testes are not externally located, and the main difference between males and females is the location of the genital aperture in relation to the umbilicus and the anus. Dugongs have two teats, one located behind each flipper. There are few differences between sexes; the body structures are almost the same. Shallow waters are used as sites for breeding and calving, minimising the risk of predation. They communicate through chirps, whistles, barks, and other sounds that echo underwater. Different sounds have been observed with different amplitudes and frequencies, implying different purposes. Visual communication is limited due to poor eyesight. Visual communication is mainly used for lekking for courtship purposes. Mothers and calves remain in almost constant physical contact, and calves have been known to reach out and touch their mothers with their flippers for reassurance.

A dugong reaches sexual maturity between the ages of eight and eighteen. Females know about male sexual maturity by observing the eruption of tusks in males. Tusk erupts in males when testosterone hormone levels reach a high level. A female usually gives birth at the age between six and ten years. However, females give birth only a few times during their life, and exhibit considerable parental care in their young.

In some populations, males may establish a territory and females in heat will visit the territory for mating. A male will try to impress the females while defending the area from other males, a practice known as lekking. In other areas many males attempt to mate with the same female, sometimes inflicting injuries to the female or each other. During this process, the female usually copulate with multiple males, who fight to mount her from below? This greatly increases the chances of conception.

Females give birth usually one calf after a 13–15 months gestation. Birth occurs in very shallow water, and almost on the shore. As soon as the young is born the mother pushes it to the surface to take a breath. Newborns are usually 1.2 metres long and weigh around 30 kg. The calf nurses for 14–18 months, although it begins to eat seagrasses soon after birth. A calf normally leaves its mother once it is matured.

Threats and Conservation

They have few natural predators, such as crocodiles, sharks, and killer whales, pose a threat to the young. A large number of infections and parasitic diseases by helminthes, cryptosporidium affect dugongs. Bacterial infections are common.

The dugong has been hunted for thousands of years for its meat and oil. The IUCN lists the dugong as a species vulnerable to extinction, while the Convention on International Trade in Endangered Species (CITES) limits or bans the trade of derived products. With its long lifespan of 70 years or more and slow rate of reproduction, the dugong is especially vulnerable to extinction. They have disappeared from the waters of Hong Kong, Mauritius, and Taiwan, as well as parts of Cambodia, Japan, the Philippines and Vietnam.

Chapter - 27

Chandigarh: Indian Grey Mongoose (Herpestes edwardsi)

Indian Grey Mongoose (Herpestes edwardsi), IUCN: LC (Least Concerned), India: Schedule II

Scientific Classification

Kingdom	:	Animalia
Phylum	:	Chordata
Class	:	Mammalia
Order	:	Carnivora
Family	:	Herpestidae
Genus	:	Herpestes
Species	:	Herpestes edwardsi

Body Structure

The Indian grey mongoose (*Herpestes edwardsi*) is a small, slender carnivore, with a long, bushy, tapering tail. It has short legs, and sharp, non-retractable claws, and with a long and pointed snout, and short, rounded ears barely protruding above head. The coat is coarse and fairly long, and greyish to light brown in colour as shown in the photo, and with the individual hairs banded black and white. The tawny grey or iron grey fur, is more grizzled and stiffer and coarser than that of other mongooses. The muzzle, cheeks, edges of the ears and feet have a rusty brown tinge. The body length varies from 36–45 cm and the body weight varies from 0.9-1.7 kg. Their tail length equals their body length.

The male is larger than the female. A number of subspecies of Indian grey mongoose are recognised. This Indian grey mongoose species is distinguished from the small Indian mongoose, *Herpestes auropunctatus*, H. javanicus by its larger size and longer, coarser reddish fur.

Ecology

The Indian grey mongoose or common grey mongoose (*Herpestes edwardsi*) is mainly found in the Indian subcontinent and in West Asia, especially in Saudi Arabia, Kuwait, Bahrain, Turkey, Iran, Afghanistan and Pakistan. They are also found in Nepal, Sri Lanka, and Bangladesh. They are commonly found in open forests, scrublands and crop fields, often close to human settlements. It lives in burrows, among groves of trees, hedgerows, and takes shelter under rocks or bushes and even in drains. It is a climber. They are usually found singly or in pairs.

Food

They prey on rodents, snakes, birds' eggs, and hatchlings, frogs, fish, lizards as well as larger prey including hares and egrets etc, and variety of invertebrates such as earthworms, grasshoppers, scorpions, centipedes, crabs, and fruits, berries, and roots. They also scavenge on waste materials near human settlements. It is omnivorous. It kills prey by biting to the neck or head. The Indian grey mongoose typically opens eggs by holding them between the paws and biting a hole in the little end. They are very inquisitive and periodically stand up with rear legs and look around for enemies. They produce a sound to alert other members of the imminent danger if any.

Reproduction

It usually mates between March and October and may breed two to three times each year. The gestation period is 60 to 65 days; the female gives birth to two to four offspring. The life span is about 12 years in captivity. It is also a pet animal of man and they are kept as pet to get rid of rats, mice and other pests from home.

Threats and Conservation

The species is protected in India. However, illegal trade for the coat of the animal for making of paint brushes and shaving brushes continues, and this is one of its most significant threats.

Chapter - 28

The State/Union Territory Animal of Delhi: Nilgai (Boselaphus tragocamelus)

Nilgai (Boselaphus tragocamelus): IUCN: LC (Least Concerned), India: Schedule II animal.

Kingdom	:	Animalia
Phylum	:	Chordata
Class	:	Mammalia
Order	:	Artiodactyla
Family	:	Bovidae
Subfamily	:	Bovinae
Genus	:	Boselaphus Peter Simon Pallas,1766, Blainville, 1816
Species	:	*Boselaphus tragocamelus*

The Nilgai or blue bull literally meaning "blue cow"; (*Boselaphus tragocamelus*) is the largest Asian antelope. The vernacular name "Nilgai" comes from the fusion of the Hindi words *nil* ("blue") and *gai* ("cow"). The word was first recorded in use in 1882. Another consideration of its origin could be from the Persian *GAW* ("cow"). Nilgai is endemic to the Indian subcontinent. Its binomial name was given by German zoologist Peter Simon Pallas in 1766. During Mughal Emperor Aurangzeb's reign (1658–1707) the Nilgai was known by the name *nilghor* ("nil" for "blue" and "ghor" for "horse") and the animal was hunted heavily for meat and skin.

Remains of the Nilgai dating back to the Pleistocene have been discovered from the Kurnool caves in southern India. Evidence suggests that they were hunted by humans for their meat, skin and horn during the Mesolithic period (about 5,000 to 8,000 years ago).

Body Structure

An adult Nilgai is a tall Antelope like horse and measures about 100-150 cm tall at the shoulder. Males weigh 109–288 kg and the females weigh 100–213 kg. The antelope is characterised by its sturdy thin-legs; a sloping back, a deep neck with a white patch on the throat, a short crest of hair along the neck terminating in a tuft, and white facial spots. They look like a cow. The head-and-body length varies between 1.7–2.1 metres. They exhibit sexual dimorphism. Females and juveniles are orange to tawny colour and Adult males are iron-grey or bluish-grey colour coat. The throat region bears a tuft of black stiff hair. Their horns are short and cone shaped. Only males possess horns measuring 15–24 centimetres long. They are very fast runners and fast running helps them to avoid carnivores.

Ecology

The Nilgai is diurnal. They prefer to stay and graze in low vegetation in hills and plains. They prefer grasses and herbs and they also eat woody plants in the dry tropical forests. They try to avoid dense forests. Nilgai are distributed all over India. In India, the Nilgai shares its habitat with the four-horned antelope, Chinkara, chital and blackbuck. The Nilgai and the Chinkara collectively prefer the area

A male Nilgai showing the face, white throat patch, beard and short horns.

rich in *Acacia* and *Butea* species. They live in groups; three distinct types of groups are usually found in the field. The groups are (i) one or two adult females with young calves, (ii) three to six adult males, few females and yearlings; (iii) all-male groups with two to 18 members. Major populations occur in the Terai lowlands in the foothills of the Himalayas. The antelope is extinct in Bangladesh and sparsely found in Nepal and Pakistan. The Nilgai has been associated with Indian culture since the Vedic period. Nilgai have been considered a pest in several north Indian states, especially in Bihar, and Uttar Pradesh as they ravage crop fields and cause considerable damage.

Reproduction

Males become sexually active when they become four or five years old. Females become sexually mature by two years of age. The male

Nilgai mark their territories by forming dung piles as much as 50 centimetres in radius. Fights take place in both sexes and involve pushing their necks against each other or ramming into one another using horns. A young male was observed making a submissive display in the Sariska Reserve by kneeling before an adult male, who stood erect (wikipedia.com). Mating season varies geographically. A peak breeding season lasts three to four months in most of the places. Gestation lasts eight to nine months. Usually, a single calf (sometimes twins or even triplets) is born. As typical of several bovid species, Nilgai calves stay hidden for the first few weeks of their lives. The lifespan of the Nilgai is about ten years.

Threats and Conservation

Natural predators of Nilgai are the tiger, lion, leopard, Dholes (generally predate juveniles) wolves and Hyenas.

Humans poach them for meat and skin and thus their numbers have been reduced. If alarmed; it flees up to 300 metres or even 700 metres, galloping away from the source of danger. The Nilgai is categorised as Least Concern by the IUCN. They are now fully protected in India by wildlife law.

Chapter - 29

Lakshadweep: Butterfly-fish (Chaetodon decussotus)

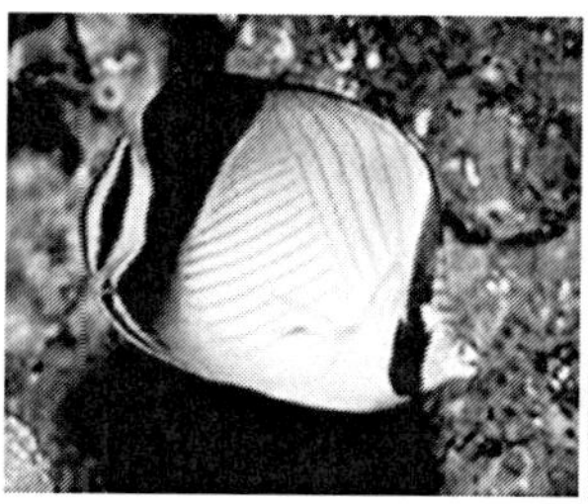

Butterfly fish (Chaetodon decussotus)

Kingdom	:	Animalia
Phylum	:	Chordata
Class	:	Actinopterygii
Order	:	Perciformes
Family	:	Chaetodontidae
Genus	:	Chaetodon
Species	:	Chaetodon decussotus

The common name butterfly refer to the brightly coloured and strikingly patterned bodies of many species.They bear shades of black, white, blue, red, orange, and yellow colour and look beautiful. Some species are dull in colour. Butterfly-fishes mostly range from 12 to 22 cm in length. They are largely found in coral reefs. After DNA sequencing, they are classified into the family Chaetodontidae. The fossil record of this group is scanty. The Chaetodontidae emerged probably in the early to mid-Eocene, and together with the few other fossils, it allows the scientific deduction that most living genera were probably originated 23 Million years ago.

Body Structure

The largest species, the lined butterfly fish and the saddle butterfly fish, C. ephippium, grow to 30 cm. Many have eyespots on their flanks and dark bands across their eyes, not unlike the patterns seen on butterfly wings. Butterfly-fish have uninterrupted dorsal fins with tail fins that may be rounded or truncated, but not forked.

Ecology

They are generally diurnal and can swim to the water depth of 18 m deep and some species descend to 180 m. They exhibit territorial behaviour and stick to particular home ranges. Some of them graze on corals, coral polyps and sea anemones and called coralivores. They usually swim in pairs and stake claim to a specific coral head. Some species live in groups and they are zooplankton feeders. By night, butterfly-fish hide in reef crevices and exhibit markedly different colouration. Their colouration also makes them popular aquarium fish. Butterfly-fishes are pelagic spawners. Butterfly-fish are found mostly on the reefs of the Atlantic, Indian, and Pacific Oceans. A number of species pairs occur in the Indian and Pacific Oceans, members of the huge genus Chaetodon. Their colouration also makes them popular aquarium fish.

Reproduction

Females release many buoyant eggs into the water, which become part of the plankton, floating with the currents until hatching.

The fry go through a stage called tholichthys stage, wherein the body of the post-larval fish is covered with large, bony plates extending from the head. The bony plates are shed as they mature.

One family of butterfly-fish called, the scats (Scatophagidae) retain the bony structure. The family name Scatophagidae derives from the

Ancient Greek words chaite ("hair") and odontos ("tooth"). This is an allusion to the rows of brush-like teeth found in their small, protrusible mouths.

Threat and Conservation

The main threat is impact of global warming leading to coral bleeching.

Human efforts to lessen the impact of global warming and take scientific steps to protect corals leading to the protection of Butterfly fish.

Chapter - 30

Puducherry: Indian Palm Squirrel (*Funambulus palmarum*)

***Indian Palm Squirrel (*Funambulus palmarum**),
India: Schedule IV animal, Cites: 7**

Kingdom	:	Animalia
Phylum	:	Chordata
Class	:	Mammalia
Order	:	Rodentia
Family	:	Sciuridae
Genus	:	*Funambulus*
Species	:	*F. palmarum*

The Indian palm squirrel (*Funambulus palmarum*) is a species of rodent in the family Sciuridae found naturally in India. *There are two species of squirrels such as one species is three striped (Funambulus palmarum) and the other is* five striped (Funambulus pennanti). Both species are found throughout India. The three striped is common in south India and the five striped ones are common in north-India. Squirrels are rodents like rats, and mice and commonly *seen in gardens and fruit orchards.* Biologists have identified four valid subspecies on the basis geographic distribution. These subspecies are (i) *Funambulus palmarum bellerica* Wrought on, 1916; (ii) *Funambulus palmarum palmarum* (Linnaeus, 1766), (iii) *Funambulus palmarum brodiei* (Blyth, 1849), (iv) *Funambulus palmarum robertsoni* Wrought on, 1916.

Body Structure

The palm squirrel has a bushy tail, slightly shorter than its body, which is about the size of a large chipmunk. The back is a grizzled, grey-brown colour with three conspicuous white stripes which run from head to tail. The two outer stripes run from the forelegs to the hind legs only. It has a creamy-white belly and a tail covered with interspersed, long, black and white or grey hair. The small ears of the squirrels are triangular. Juvenile squirrels have significantly lighter colouration, which gets darker as they grow old. Albino squirrels are rare.

Ecology

Their teeth, especially the four incisors in both jaws are well adapted for gnawing all types of vegetative food; shoots, buds, bark, fruits, nuts and bird *eggs. The teeth grow throughput their life.* Their vocalisation is limited to sounds like "chip chip chip" when danger is present. Indian palm squirrel does not hibernate in winter or aestivate in summer. They have invaded urban areas and are domesticated and trained to accept food from humans.

Social Relevance in India

A legend explains the stripes on the back of the squirrels. During the construction of the Rama Setu (bridge) at Rameswaram by Lord Rama and his Vanara Sena, a little squirrel rolled in the beach sand and then ran to the end of the bridge to shake off the sand from its back (chanting Lord Rama's name all along). Sri Rama, pleased by the creature's dedication, caressed the squirrel's back and ever since, the Indian squirrel carried white stripes on its back, which are believed to be the mark of Sri Rama's fingers. Therefore, Indian Palm Squirrel is loved by Indians.

Reproduction

Breeding takes place in grass nests during the autumn. The gestation period is 34 days. Litters of two or three are common. The young are weaned after about 10 weeks and become sexually mature at 9 months. Adult weight is 100 g. Much is not known about their longevity, but one specimen lived 5.5 years in captivity.

A nest of Indian palm squirrel

Threats and Conservation

The natural predators are game birds, leopards and other wild cats.

Their conservation depends upon protection of their habitats.

References

Dash, M.C. and S.P. Dash. 2009. Fundamentals of Ecology, McGraw-Hill Publications, New Delhi, 562 p.

Discovering Wildlife: the Ultimate Fact File, Reader's Digest of India. Google.com.search

Ministry of Environment, Forests Climate Change, New Delhi Publications.

Nayar, S. M. 1992. Indian Endangered Animals and their Conservation, (In Odia, 1995), National Book Trust of India, New Delhi, 96 p.

Rao, Jagannatha, A.N.1991. Atlas to India's Wildlife, TT.Maps & Publication Ltd, Madras, 95 p.

Wikipedia, the free encyclopedia (Mammals, National Parks and other animals).

Zoological Survey of India- Book (2016) on Scheduled Mammals of India: Issue of Endangerment of Species.

Index